WHAT KIND OF LOVE IS THIS?

What Kind of Love is This?

"For God so loved that He gave"

Dr. Susan Marie Pender

Christian International Publishing
Santa Rosa Beach, Florida

Copyright © 2018 by Susan Marie Pender.
All rights reserved.
This book or parts thereof may not be reproduced in any form, stored in a retrieval system, or transmitted in any form by any means—electronic, mechanical, photocopy, recording, or otherwise—without prior written permission of the publisher, except as provided by United States of America copyright law.

Christian International Publishing
177 Apostles Way
Santa Rosa Beach, Florida 32459 www.cipublishing.org

ISBN: 978-1-7325703-9-9
Published August 2018
Printed in the United States of America

Scripture quotations taken from Thompson ChainReference Bible New International Version Copyright 1990 by The B.B. Kirkbride Bible Company, Inc. Indianapolis, Indiana.

Holy Bible, New International Version®, NIV® Copyright ©1973, 1978, 1984, 2011 by Biblica, Inc.® Used by permission.

For speaking engagements or questions, e-mail Contact Susan Marie Pender
Susanmariepender@gmail.com
www.lilyofthevalleyhealing.com

Acknowledgments

I acknowledge Father God for loving and for pursuing us until we surrendered our hearts to Him. I am thankful for the grace He gives us and for the kind fatherly attributes He constantly shows us. He pursues us no matter who we are, where we are, or what wrong things we have done.

I acknowledge Reverend Clifford Deeton, our family's pastor at Westminster Presbyterian Church of Baker, Minnesota for being a wonderful, caring friend and providing oversight to our family with wisdom and integrity. You helped my family find purpose and meaning for our lives. You were steadfast in your character and lead by being an example to us.

Thank you, Lauren Peterson, for being a genuine, kind, loving family friend and neighbor over a lifetime. Thank you for supporting my father and our family during a time of intervention in all of our lives. Without your support and dedication, many lives would have never changed.

I am grateful for the Tuesday evening Bible study that I attended for twelve years. These were held at the home of Gladys Jacobson in Fertile, Minnesota. Without fail, Gladys opened her home every week, year after year, to anyone wanting to come to fellowship, sing songs in worship, study the Bible, and pray together. She provided a loving, warm atmosphere, with homemade donuts and pastries that we ate while around her table. She loved her family and community so much. She desired for them to all know Jesus Christ as their savior and to know the goodness and kindness of the Lord in each of their lives.

Contents

God Pursues Me with His Love 5

Dad, I Love You! 11

Alcohol Took the Place of a 17

Father's Love 17

Removing Past Mistakes Through Forgiveness.................. 21

Holy Spirit, I Need You 29

Impartation Through Laying on of Hands 39

God Still Heals People Today 45

Angels or Another Spirit 55

An Evening Bible Study at My Neighbor's House 75

Better Put This on the Shelf... 81

It Was the Holy Spirit 85

"This is That, That is This" 89

What Does This Mean?.. 95

What Must We Do? 95

Something Big is Coming 99

Peace I Leave with You .... **Error! Bookmark not defined.**

What Kind of Love is This?

Endnotes .... **Error! Bookmark not defined.**

More from the Author .... **Error! Bookmark not defined.**

Introduction

Everyone is born with a plan and a purpose for their lives. This is found in Jeremiah 29:11.

For I know the plans I have for you, plans to prosper you and not to harm you, plans to give you hope and a future.
Jeremiah 29:11, NIV

The time and place we are born is purposeful and even planned by God. This is in Psalm 139:16.

"Your eyes saw my unformed body. All the days ordained for me were written in your book before one of them came to be.
Psalm 139:16, NIV

Therefore, every person will at some point in life, ask this question, "What is my purpose in life?"

Only God has those answers because He is the one who wrote them in your book before you came into your family on the earth.

Many people attend church, are involved in various good organizations, serve as good neighbors living good lives, but still miss out on fulfilling the purpose for their lives because they haven't received the one who loved them and died for them so they might live an abundant life. Jesus Christ is the way, and the truth and the life. No one comes to the Father except through Him.

All of your acceptance, value, security, and your purpose in life comes from the one who created you in the beginning.

Without knowing God's fatherly love toward us as His sons and daughters, we will not possess the confidence and security necessary to live our lives to the fullest. Without knowing God's love through our parents and those we are in a relationship with, our identities will be skewed, and we will not feel valued as God intended for us to feel.

At different times in life, I have questioned my purpose and what I was supposed to be doing. Each time I sought this out, God answered me. He loved me so much that He kept me safe when I was on a wrong path, and He kept pursuing me until He won my heart and devotion. No person wants to live life without some meaning to it and without giving and receiving genuine love.

God sees everything in our life and has not left us all alone to walk it out. He knows the place we live and the family we are placed in when we came into the earth through our mother's

Introduction

womb. All of God's promises will help us overcome every obstacle that keeps us from receiving His love for us and from giving this same love freely to others. He promises to never leave us. Take His hand today and receive Him into your heart so you can fulfill every purpose and every dream that is inside of you.

What Kind of Love is This?

One

God Pursues Me with His Love

When I was a senior in high school, I began asking the Lord questions about my life. Sometimes I would drive our family's second car to school in the early morning because of participation in after-school events. Living in the country ten miles from town, I would leave home a little early, so I had time to stop at my family's church in a small village about three miles from my home. There, I would ask God for some answers to my many questions.

The church doors were always open in the early mornings when I arrived and there was never anyone inside. Hoping to be alone, I would peek in the doorway of the pastor's office but never did see him there. I would go into the sanctuary and just sit in a pew surrounded by the pretty environment and silence. I sat alone and talked to God there.

In the early morning while sitting in this church, I felt close to God and asked Him questions about my life. There seemed to be so many things I didn't understand about growing up, being an adult, and what I was supposed to do in my life. I didn't know who else to talk to. Somehow, I knew God heard everything I said, and it gave me comfort to share my thoughts and concerns with Him.

My family went to church every Sunday. My mom taught the little children's Sunday school, and my dad was a deacon. My siblings and I were all baptized and confirmed in this Presbyterian Church. I learned many Bible stories there, but I don't remember ever hearing that we could have a personal relationship with God. In church, God was presented as a distant being, not as someone who was personal and active in our lives today. I always believed in God, but I did not know Him in a personal way.

In my senior year, to help us make career choices, we took aptitude tests to determine our strengths and weaknesses. My scores were so low across the board that they couldn't offer me any career direction. All I remember our school counselor saying to me was, "Sorry." I believe this was the stress I was experiencing in my home.

With four brothers and one sister, I always had someone to play with and someone to talk to. We were always entertaining family and friends and preparing large meals, but there was something in our home that was emotionally crippling for all of us. My father was an alcoholic.

His personality would change when he drank, and our home would become unsafe and insecure. I had a lot of insecurities and mixed messages of who I was because of the things I experienced in my home.

After graduation, I got a dietary position at a hospital in Fargo, North Dakota and moved there. In a hurry to move out of my home, I married a year later and moved 1500 miles away. I knew so little then about how to do life well.

The man I married had just returned from Vietnam and had many unresolved problems. He was restless and would not live in one place very long, so we moved often. By the time I was twenty-three, I began questioning my purpose in life again, and even my identity.

God Pursues Me with His Love

At my workplace, I began asking an older woman, whom I worked alongside, questions about what it meant to be a Christian.

I asked her questions like, "How do you know you are a Christian?" Then I would ask her, "How do you become a Christian?" Then I would ask her, "Why do some people say they are a Christian, but their lives do not look like they are a Christian?" Then I wondered why some people act like they are a Christian, but they are quiet and don't say anything about their faith, so you cannot be sure of where their peace comes from.

This woman never gave me any answers that satisfied my questions. I just seemed to have more questions every day. I wanted this peace that some people seemed to have, but I just wasn't sure what it was that they had or how I could get it.

I grew up going to church every Sunday and did all the right things that I thought a Christian should do. I wasn't a bad person and hadn't done anything really horrible in my life other than making some wrong decisions, but I knew there was something missing in my life. I felt these answers were buried somewhere and I was seeking to find them.

Alone in my apartment one evening, I heard Billy Graham speaking on the television. He was talking about what it meant to be a Christian. In another room, I quickly went to the television to hear what this man had to say. He was explaining why some people appear to be Christians just because they go to church. He said they are not Christians if they have never received Jesus Christ as their Savior. Graham said we can have religion by going to church and we can do all the right things, but if we don't have a relationship with Jesus Christ, then all the things we do in the church and in our lives are meaningless.

Billy Graham said that the only way to have this peace in our hearts was to have Jesus Christ in our hearts. The world cannot give us this peace. It can only come from Jesus Christ.

This man answered all of the questions I had been asking over the past several months. What I needed was a Savior. I needed the love of a God that was able to wash my sins away and make me whole.

Billy Graham went on to explain that this was a free gift, and all I needed to do was to receive this gift called Jesus. I sat intensely close to the television, soaking in every word that he said.

The Lord prepared my heart during these prior months by causing me to question who God was and how I could know Him. I knew God only from reading about Him in the Bible and did not have a personal relationship with Him.

It was the Holy Spirit that aroused my heart's longing to know God in a personal way. Then God set a time and a place to meet with me. I was alone in my apartment in March of 1976. God answered all of my questions through this man Billy Graham. God pursues us with His love and kindness. He definitely had been pursuing me.

Now the Lord had me in a place where He had my undivided attention and could speak to me so I could know Him personally.

Here God would answer all my questions, and I could come to know Him personally as my Lord and Savior. The Bible says,

God Pursues Me with His Love

It is the goodness of God that leads us to repentance.
Romans 2:4, NIV

Repent means to change our thinking and actions. I t i s His kindness and love that draw us to Him.

I prayed from my heart to receive Jesus Christ into my life and felt changed in an instant. I was so excited. I knew that when I prayed with Billy Graham that day, I became a different person. Everything inside of me had changed and was new. Romans 10:9-10 says,

If you will confess with your mouth the Lord Jesus and will believe in your heart that God raised him from the dead you will be saved. For with the heart man believes unto righteousness and with the mouth confession is made unto salvation.

Romans 10:9-10, NIV

I wanted to tell everyone what had happened to me, but I didn't even understand what had actually happened. I had never heard this message of receiving Jesus Christ as my Savior and didn't know where a church was that talked about this kind of a message.

I began reading my Bible and talking to God like he was my closest friend. During one of my quiet times with the Lord, I heard Him speak to me, in a gentle soft voice. He told me to speak to my father and tell him that I loved him.

I was planning to go home for a weekend visit, and during this visit God wanted me to tell my father I loved him. This seemed silly to me because I didn't understand why or what it would mean to my father. I had never heard my father tell me that he loved me, but now God wanted me to say this to my father.

I realized that I no longer had any bad feelings deep inside my heart toward my father like I used to. Now, I had the ability to tell him that I really did love him. Unknown to me, God was getting ready to encounter my father with love. It would be an encounter with God's love that would change
the course of his life forever and the course of the lives of my family and generations to come.

Two

Dad, I Love You!

My father's body was beginning to show signs of health problems due to his alcoholic lifestyle. His eyes and skin looked jaundiced from liver damage. While I was planning to visit my parent's home on the coming weekend, God had put it on my heart to tell my father that I loved him.

In our home, we never talked about loving each other when I was growing up. My parents took good physical care of us and instinctively I knew they loved me. I just don't remember hearing these words spoken to me or expressed verbally between my parents to each other. There were no hugs, kisses, or love words exchanged between any of us in the home. Because of the lack of displayed affection and love in my home, this request from God seemed like a big deal to me. It wasn't natural for me to speak and act like this "*love stuff*" around my family or anyone.

I think God put a measure of grace in my heart when He asked me to do this because there was no fear or reservation in me. It felt more like I was delivering a gift.

For so many years my dad's drinking behavior bothered me because he was never able or willing to stop the bad behavior that came with the alcohol. I also knew him as a kind person and one who provided many great experiences for us, such as huge family gatherings, animals to show at the county and state fair, and picnics at the lakes on Sundays. He taught me how to spear fish in an icehouse and drive farm equipment with him.

I felt that he was locked in an addiction and didn't have the key to open this lock and escape. When God told me to tell my father I loved him, it was like a deposit was placed inside me that I needed to release. It felt like I was pregnant with an urgent message and would remain pregnant with it until I released it to him.

I had no idea how this was all going to take place but somehow had peace that God would help me. I had every intention without any reservation of talking to my dad. After giving my heart to Jesus as my Lord, I realized I did not fear my father anymore but instead had something to say to him.

When going home for this weekend visit, I was attentive to hear God's leading as to when and how to speak to my father. I kept looking and listening for the right opportunity.

As I rode in the back seat of their car to church with my parents that Sunday morning in June of 1976, I leaned forward preparing to speak to my dad about the message stirring inside of me. I heard a small, gentle voice within me that said, "No, not now."

I relaxed back into my comfortable position alone in the back seat. I felt peace inside me that this was going to all work out. So, I continued to listen for that gentle leading of the Lord to help me release this message welling up inside me.

I had waited for many years to confront my father in some way. While living a long distance away, I would call home just to see if he had stopped drinking and if it was safe for me to return home. It never was. Now God had come into my life, changed my attitude, and the way I viewed many things, and had prepared me to express the desire for my father's life to change. God waited until someone had the right key to unlock my father's heart. The key was God's love. I was given God's love when I repented of my own sins and became born again.

That Sunday in June, all ten of my family members sat around our dining room table for dinner. After we finished eating and visiting, everyone left the table.

Most of my family members went outside to enjoy the warm summer weather. One sibling went into the living room to watch television. Another went upstairs to lie down for a nap. I went into the kitchen to wash dishes with my sister and my mother.

Upon turning toward the dining room, I saw my father still sitting at the head of the table. He was the only one sitting at the large table. He was not talking to anyone or looking at anything. He was just sitting there. This really caught my attention. Normally, he would sit in his chair in the living room or go right outside to work. He never just sat at the table like he had nothing to do.

Taking a second look, he was still just sitting there at the table, but this time I saw a faint shadow of someone very large standing behind him. I had never seen anything like this before. I realized God must had sent an angel to help me.

I understood immediately that this was an angel and could see its upper extremities or arms and hands were over my father's shoulders. I knew God had this angel here to hold my father in his chair so I could come talk to him. When I saw this angel, I heard the Lord say to me, "Go now."

What Kind of Love is This?

Immediately, I went to my father's right side and knelt next to him. As I began to open my mouth, a flood of contained emotions poured out in tears. This was a man whom I had once feared because of things I saw him do when he had been drinking. I realized that I didn't have this fear anymore and all the negative feelings about him had left me. Now, all I felt toward my father was love.

I said, "I love you." The words just poured out of me. I began to cry. I said again, "Dad, I love you." My father began crying also.

My sister, who had been in the kitchen, came to his other side and knelt to speak the same words. I had never shared with her anything about what I was planning to do or to say. She began repeating the same words. "Yeah dad, we love you." As quickly as she responded to the unfolding display, she too was crying with heartfelt compassion.

My mother disappeared into the bathroom. She began crying too because the environment was filled with such a genuine display of love toward a man who probably felt the least deserving. I did not share with my mother the intentions I had. All I knew was what God had told me during my quiet time in my apartment, and I obeyed. I did not share my intent with anyone because I didn't even know what I was going to do.

When we deliver a message that God gives us, He will show up. There was such a sweet presence of the Lord there with all of us. I told my father that he was important to me, and I wanted him to live. We all continued crying.

I didn't know what to say next, but I heard myself ask him to stop drinking so he could live. My sister echoed the

Dad, I Love You!

same request. We pleaded with him to stop drinking so he could live to see his grandchildren. We wanted him to know his grandchildren and have a full life.

My father managed to verbalize that he knew he was dying. The excessive alcohol use caused the sclera of his eyes to look a jaundice-yellow color where they should have been white, and his facial skin was taking on a jaundice color also.

He said he just wanted to be buried behind the barn with his cows. His cows may have been the only thing alive that he could deeply relate to and verbalize his feelings to because animals only listen and pose no threat.

Because of his drinking behavior, he had damaged his relationship with the members of his family. There were walls of offenses between him and his wife, his children, possibly other extended family members, and some people in the community.

After more crying and pleading for him to stop drinking, I left to begin my journey back home. My father was bewildered for the remainder of the day, thinking about what had taken place at the dining room table; so was I. I didn't know it would be so emotionally dramatic and impactful.

After arriving home, I called my mother on the phone to see how she and my father were. She was touched by the sweetness of love that day. It brought a release of emotional pain bound within her. My father had gone to his machinery building where he sat in his chair for the remainder of the day to think about what had happened between him, his daughters and possibly even God.

This is what love looks like. It not only comforts others, but it also confronts others in a way that causes

What Kind of Love is This?

their hearts to open up to the pain they have inside. God wants to heal everyone's broken heart and restore damaged relationships. God created the family and wants to restore families. Only genuine love can mend people's hearts.

Three

Alcohol Took the Place of a Father's Love

In just one month I had given my life to the Lord, heard God's voice directing me to give a message to someone, saw an angel, and shared with someone close to me God's love for them.

It was a year later that I received a call from their pastor to join them for a designated meeting with my father. A family friend, Lauren Peterson would also be present. A family intervention was being planned to confront my father's drinking addiction and the need for medical help. We would be meeting at my parent's home without my father's prior knowledge.

When the evening arrived, we gathered one by one in their living room. My father always like having company, but he could sense by those arriving that this was not an ordinary visit. He highly esteemed his friend Lauren and had a good relationship with their pastor. I was there along with one of my brothers.

The nature of the visit could be discerned by the people who were present, but there was a calm and a peace in the room.

Our pastor explained our concern for my father's health and his destructive behavior when drinking alcohol. We acknowledged his jaundice symptoms brought on by his alcohol addiction. We reminded him of how short his life would be if he continued this type of lifestyle.

I shared that I could not come home to visit him anymore if he continued to drink and that his behaviors were too difficult for me to be around. I shared with him that I would not be able to bring his grandchildren to see him unless I knew he would be sober. My mom shared that she would not be able to continue to live with him if he did not stop drinking because of the change in his character when he drank.

Our pastor had already contacted an alcohol recovery center near us in order to obtain requirements for admission into their program and to help us understand the counseling process all of our family would be involved in. We encouraged my father to consent to his own admission. There he would receive six to eight weeks of in-hospital counseling individually and with our family. Family members were encouraged to receive counseling along with the person in recovery.

Our pastor told my father that he would take him to that hospital that very evening and he could not wait until tomorrow to make a decision. He would have to pack a suitcase and go there that night.

If he chose not to go, then my mother would be leaving and would not return. Listening to all of us share with him, in a kind loving manner, he did not feel threatened, and he understood our support for a changed life and also our desire to help him. He already had an imprint on his heart, the undeniable love of God that had caused him to break down in tears a year ago at his dining room table. He was given a choice to receive medical help and the support of others in making a life altering decision. If not, he would lose his health, his relationships, possibly his agricultural business, and die a premature death. This doesn't seem like a difficult decision to make, but when alcohol or a drug or

Alcohol Took the Place of a Father's Love

any type of addiction has power over a person, one feels powerless to make this decision.

The choices were presented calmly and clearly. My father agreed that he would go with our pastor and his friend Lauren to the recovery center. I sensed my father was almost relieved that someone cared enough to reach out to help him.

People display this tough kind of love when they care about others. It was a decision he was not able to make on his own. He did not know help was available to him. Sometimes people need an ultimatum to make changes.

Packing his bags, he submitted to the help being offered. It was at this facility that my father was able to talk about the difficult things in life, as well as the actions that brought hurt to others.

Being in the agricultural business, a major decision to stop growing potatoes and to begin growing sugar beets had been made a few years prior. This was a new crop to their area and required a large investment in new machinery. It would take several successful crop years to pay off the debt incurred with this venture.

Obviously, it would not be beneficial for his business to have his life cut short. It also would have been difficult to financially transfer this family business at this early stage of financial investment.

At this recovery center, he was given an opportunity to express things that were painful to him. My father was ten years old during the great depression and World War II when his dad died of pneumonia, leaving nine young children for my grandmother to raise. My father stopped attending school at age ten to work on their family farm. There was no presence of a father in his life. He did not receive the instruction and support of a father. His childhood was replaced by hard work and responsibility. My father began using alcohol at a young age. This replaced the love of a father that he never had.

Four

Removing Past Mistakes Through Forgiveness

A need to be loved lies behind all addiction. Physically, when we do not feel loved, it can cause a decrease in the hormone's serotonin and dopamine. These hormones cause us to feel balanced in our mood. They are the *feel good* hormones, which are regulated in our brains by our thoughts and feelings.[1]

When we do not feel loved, we will look for something else to make us *feel good* or take the place of *unmet love*. This unmet love can be replaced by alcohol, certain drugs, unhealthy relationships, pornography, and eating disorders. Anything outside of God's safe boundaries that takes the place of love can become an addiction.[2]

After encountering God's love at the dining room table that Sunday, Dad's heart was softened. When confronted by family and friends to receive help to change addictive behaviors, he surrendered his will because he had been touched by a genuine love.

God created us so that when we love Him and love ourselves and others, our body releases the proper hormones into our systems to make us feel good. It keeps our bodies in balance. Love is a chemical fix that comes from God.

At one of our family counseling sessions, my dad stood in front of each of his family members who were present that day and asked us individually to forgive him for the wrong things he had done. It was a memorable event for me. My sister, a brother, mom and I were all present along with the chaplain and a counselor.

As my dad spoke to each one of us, telling us he was sorry for the harmful actions and words toward us when he was drinking, tears welled up within us. We were not told before our family counseling session that this was going to take place. My father was to a place in his life that he realized the harm he had caused all of us when he had gone into a drunken state over and over again.

He had threatened my mother's life many times and caused my siblings and myself to find a place to hide in fear until morning when the environment would become calm again. We all had an opportunity to stand face-to-face and eye-to-eye with him while he poured out his heart of sorrow for the pain and torment delivered to us when he was intoxicated.

When one family member acknowledged that they forgave him, he stepped to the next family member and began from the beginning again with that person. He waited for an acknowledgment from each family member that they understood the depth of his repentance and his love for each one of us.

Each one of us forgave and released him from all past wrongful words and actions toward us. As we all released forgiveness, the pain in our hearts dissipated also. My father took responsibility for his harmful actions and thereby became free of the guilt that weighed heavily upon him.

Removing Past Mistakes Through Forgiveness

Talking with him one day alone in his room, he told me he had accepted Jesus Christ as his savior and that he had not ever known a time in his life that he felt so glad inside.

Because God had intimately met with my dad that June day in 1976 at his dining room table with an outward display of love that was unexpected and undeserved, he was able to trust God enough to open up his heart and receive Jesus Christ as his savior a year later. Because my dad knew the debt of sin that God forgave him of, and that God still had an overwhelming love for him, he was able to reach out to each one of his family members with a heart of humility and show that same love by confessing his sin to us.

I had three brothers who were not able to participate in any of the counseling sessions because they were in the armed services. One brother was in the Navy and two were in the Army all stationed in Germany at this time. They did not know our father was in treatment for alcohol addiction and that our family was attending counseling sessions.

Several months after being released from treatment, my parents made a trip to Germany. I did not know until many years later that their purpose in traveling to Germany was so my father could talk to these three sons and tell them of his addiction recovery. My father had received more than a recovery from alcohol addiction; he received a changed heart through his repentance and acceptance of Jesus Christ as his savior.

My father wanted to tell his other three sons that he was sorry for all the wrong things he had done while drinking during the time they were children growing up. He wanted to tell them he was sorry for yelling at them and yelling at their mother and causing so much chaos and fighting in our home. He wanted to take responsibility for the pain he caused them, and he wanted to ask for their forgiveness. My father wanted to take responsibility for the pain he caused his sons while in that destructive environment. He spoke separately to each of them letting them know he was very sorry for hurting them emotionally and mentally and that he was wrong for treating them so harshly. He also told each one that he loved them.

One of my brothers told me many years later that while our parents were in Germany, his father talked to him for two hours, telling him about all the changes he made in his life. This brother stated, "My dad came all the way across the world to tell me he was sorry for hurting me, and that he loved me!"

This brother said he knew after his dad was done talking to him, that any problems he had were his own. He could no longer blame his father for his own bad choices.

This brother eventually went through alcohol treatment and never drank alcohol again. He had the courage to change his lifestyle because of the love and forgiveness extended to him by his father.

This is what Jesus Christ did for all of us. He came all the way from heaven to earth, because of his love for us and paid the debt for every man's sins. Receiving Jesus Christ made a way for each person to come back into fellowship with God as their heavenly Father and made a way for families to be restored.

When my father drank alcohol, he caused arguing and violence in our home. This caused much tension for everyone. Our home situation did not teach us to live in harmony with one another or to have healthy relationships

Removing Past Mistakes Through Forgiveness

with other people. Only forgiveness and love can heal our hearts and cause our homes to be places of safety and security.

People in our community could see there was a change in my father. However, he only talked with those close to him about how God came into his life in a loving way. He never spoke publicly about this.

At this time, a cousin was having difficulty in his marriage because drinking alcohol was an escape from problems in his life. A lcohol abuse was a lifestyle also observed in his home. When my cousin talked with my father about the counseling, he received to help overcome that addiction, he desired to do the same. My cousin was so encouraged that he was also able to lay down his alcohol addiction also. This changed the course of his life.

A second cousin visited with my father after recovery and shared with me many years later, that my father expressed to him that he would not have entered treatment for recovery if his daughters had not shared their love with him that day. This love touched my father's heart giving him a reason to live.

The jaundice condition disappeared because there was no more alcohol coming into his body. This allowed his liver to heal and function properly. He was able to recover his health and live another thirty years.

God restored his life which allowed him valuable time to prosper in business and to be influential in the lives of his grandchildren. After receiving Jesus Christ as his savior, he was able to stop his destructive, addictive behavior.

The future for my dad was altered. His demeanor changed and attitude changed. He was happier to be alive because now there was something to look forward to in life.

Each new day became a good experience.

Because he no longer went to the same places that he had gone to in the past, his circle of friends changed. There was no more waking up in the morning feeling guilty for what was done or said the night before. With peace in their home, my parents now talked and discussed issues. The smoking of large fat cigars, and cigarettes also stopped. There was an entire lifestyle change.

Because of God's love coming into a life, a heart became open to an entire lifestyle change. This decision caused an extension of life. It allowed a life to prosper mentally, relationally, spiritually, and financially.

He was able to financially secure his agriculture business and pass this inheritance to his children and grandchildren. He was able to live to know his grandchildren and experience life with them and also to leave a legacy for them. This is prosperity.

God's love can give you an inheritance while you are on earth, and give you a place in heaven for eternity. You only need to receive it.

With all these changes happening in my own life, I felt it was important to be in fellowship with others who desired to study Scripture. I began looking for a church where I could study the Bible and learn more about this God of love. Eventually, after attending several churches, I found a woman's Bible study that met on Tuesday evenings, where I felt a connection.

There was a sweet presence of the Lord among these young women. I loved to be with them. I listened to the

Removing Past Mistakes Through Forgiveness

Scripture readings and went home to study for myself so I could know more about this wonderful relationship that I had begun to experience with God.

What Kind of Love is This?

Five

Holy Spirit, I Need You

The women's Bible Study that I attended on Tuesday evenings was a heavenly gift for me. The girls I met there had something different that I had not found in the organized church. I wasn't sure what it was at the time, but whatever it was, there was life there.

Two of the women had already attended and graduated from a Bible college. I would listen intently to how they talked about Scripture and then I would search out the scriptures for myself when I got home. I knew this was where God wanted me to be, at least for now.

When these women prayed, they would talk to God, find a Scripture to correspond with the prayer need, then pray the Scripture out loud. In this process, they would pray in words I didn't understand. It was like these words were just between them and God.

They later explained to me they had received the baptism in the Holy Spirit, and that is why they had this prayer language. I had never heard of a prayer language before, but I sensed God's peace on it. This praying in an unknown tongue did witness inside of me that it was something that was of God, even though I didn't understand it with my natural mind.

When I asked them about this language, they explained to me it was something they received when they were baptized in the Holy Spirit. They suggested I read the book of Acts and ask God to answer my questions. So, I did. At night before going to bed, I would read the book of Acts, just a few scriptures each night. I would take my time to hear what God was saying to me in the scriptures. I took them seriously when they told me to ask God what I was reading.

In the church I grew up in, I was not taught to read my Bible and ask God questions as I read it. I thought they were just stories about history, but now I realized there were applicable for me today. After I gave my heart to Jesus Christ, the words in the Bible spoke to me. There was life in them. They meant something to me. I asked God to show me the truth about what I was reading in the book of Acts.

In our Bible study, we would sing simple songs to God, love on Him and worship Him with these simple songs. These young women would sing with words I could understand, then they would sing in a heavenly language that I did not understand. I was only able to worship God in my own understanding, and I really wanted to be able to worship God from my spirit also. It was like I could only go so deep in my adoration, and there was a deeper adoration that I was not able to experience with God. So, I was beginning to have a desire for more of God so I could express to Him how I felt in a more meaningful way.

In August of 1982, a woman by the name of Sarah Jerick came to speak in our little town. She spoke about how to have a victorious life. She said it was through the baptism of the Holy Spirit that we can walk in victory in our Christian life.

Holy Spirit, I Need You

For John baptized with water, but in a few days, you will be baptized with the Holy Ghost.
Acts 1:5, NIV

This is the baptism of the Holy Spirit. When a person receives this baptism, they are empowered to be a witness of
God's character. This is stated in Acts 1:8,

But you will receive power when the Holy Spirit comes on you and you will be my witnesses in Jerusalem and in all Judea and Samaria and to the ends of the earth.
Acts 1:8, NIV

After Jesus was taken up into Heaven, the Holy Spirit could come to earth. On the day of Pentecost, described in Acts 2, the Holy Spirit came suddenly into the upper room where the disciples and others were told to wait. In verse 2 it says that they were all filled with the Holy Spirit and began to speak with other tongues as the Spirit gave them utterance.

I knew this was something God wanted me to have. So, when Sarah Jerick came to speak in our little town, I had a good understanding of what she was teaching with regard to the Holy Spirit according to the book of Acts.

When Sarah finished speaking, she offered to pray for anyone wo wanted to receive this baptism. I asked Sarah to pray for me to receive this gift of Holy Spirit. God offers this gift to all of us; in fact, God commands us to receive this baptism in the Holy Spirit described in Acts.

On one occasion while he was eating with them he gave them this command: "Do not leave Jerusalem but wait for the gift my Father promised which you have heard me speak about."

Acts 1:4, NIV

I had studied the book of Acts for myself and asked God to help reveal it to me. Then I received this same teaching about the Holy Spirit in the book of Acts from Sarah. It all aligned with what I had learned for myself. Now I was ready to receive this Holy Spirit with an understanding of what I was asking for.

Sarah asked Jesus to baptize me with the Holy Spirit, and by faith I made a sound. This sound I formulated did not come from my head. It wasn't anything that I thought to speak. The sound came out of my belly. It was the most beautiful sound and language. It was time to leave, so I went outside where I was alone with God. I was speaking in an unknown tongue, talking to the God of the universe personally. As I got into my car, I remember saying to God for the first time, "Abba Father."

This came out of a deeper place of my heart of knowing Him. Abba means "*papa or daddy.*" I knew God was always with me in my home and at work and wherever I went, but now it was like I came into another deeper measure of knowing Him and His presence with me. I just felt a little closer to Him and closer to His heart. Now I knew Him in a more intimate way as a Father with love towards me.

God is a spirit, and we are also a spirit being. We are a spiritual being who has a soul, which is our mind, will, and emotions, and we live in a physical body. We can worship God in the spirit through this language that is received through the baptism of the Holy Spirit. Some things we can

Holy Spirit, I Need You

only access from God through the spirit because God is a spirit and we are spirit. The devil does not want us to have this because the devil does not understand this language. The devil is at a disadvantage when we talk to God this way.

I drove home that night praying in tongues all the way home. After arriving home, I sat in my car not wanting to go into my house because I was having so much fun praying in my heavenly language. If I went into my house, I would have to stop and concentrate on other things.

It was so wonderful to feel so close to God this way. I knew I could pray to Him anytime I wanted in this way. I just didn't want this first love experience to end by stepping into my house and having to stop praying like this. His presence felt so sweet to me. It was like a fresh drink of water that I had never tasted before. My only desire was to know Him more deeply, and to walk close to Him, and to be able to love Him more intimately.

I became very interested in prayer while attending this women's Bible study. I realized that Satan is the one who wants to bring destruction into our lives. God wants to be a Father to us and I wanted to know more about Him.

I worked full-time as a nurse, was expecting to have a baby in a few months, and was in a difficult marriage, so there were many things that attempted to pull me away from spending time with God. I soon realized I could simply spend time praying in this new language for people whom God would put on my heart while I was at home doing daily tasks and while I was at work. Praying didn't take any of my time away from doing what I needed to do.

I began to live this type of intercessor prayer lifestyle. I wanted to expose Satan and his darkness and bring God into people's lives by just praying for them in the privacy of my home. No one needed to know who I was, and I didn't need to go to a mission field. I was already living in a mission field in my home and at my place of work.

Any advances in the Kingdom of God are made in prayer. People who come to know Jesus and get saved or healed have someone behind the scene praying them into the family of God. This was now the direction my life would take, and it was my only goal in life.

It was exciting to be with God and my life had become very exciting after receiving the baptism of the Holy Spirit. I was lonely in my marriage and was not able to be around my family very much, but being with God like this made up for much of the loneliness I felt. Nothing is ever wasted when you spend it on God; whether it is time or money, He will put it to good use.

Not able to go home to visit my family very often, they were not aware of the difficulty I was experiencing, thus there was little emotional support. Having moved and relocated often, I had not established lasting friendships. Now, the only one thing that remained a constant in my life, that had any encouragement or value to me was God. He was the one I talked to, and the one I leaned on, and the one who answered all of my questions to the best that I could hear, and the best that I could understand from Scripture.

When Jesus went to Heaven, He said that He was not going to leave us alone. He said that the Holy Spirit would be with us. Most of us have a pretty easy time believing in God and that God created man and everything on the earth. Many of us believe that Jesus is the son of God and that He came to earth to die for our sins. But it seems more difficult for people to believe that there is a person called Holy Spirit, who is here with us today, and that we can walk and talk with Him every day.

The triune God is three in one. This is a mystery to understand. There is God the Father, Jesus the son of God, and the Holy Spirit. Jesus sits at the right hand of the Father in heaven. The Holy Spirit is here with us on earth to comfort us, to guide us, to counsel us, to fill us, and to be our helper.

He is those rivers of living water that we can drink from. He is the breath of air that we breathe. He is the mighty sound from Heaven as a hurricane wind. He is the bright light as of fire. He is the suddenly sound that comes from Heaven. He is the gentle nudge we feel in God's presence. He is the sweet fragrance that we can smell. We should be able to experience God with all five of our senses. We should be able to touch, smell, taste, hear and see this God who created us.

If you have never received Jesus Christ as your savior by inviting Him into your life, you can do that right now. I would like to pray for you. If you would also like to receive the baptism of the Holy Spirit just like the120 people did on the day of Pentecost, let's ask for that too.

Father in Heaven, I believe that Jesus Christ is your son….that He came to earth as a man . . . that He died for all of my sins . . . that He went to hell for three days and then rose from the dead. I believe that Jesus paid for my sins so I could be free. I want to receive you Jesus into my heart and into my life right now. Thank you that I am a child of God and that I now belong to your family, and I have an eternal home in heaven with you.

What Kind of Love is This?

When Jesus went to Heaven, He said He would not leave us alone. Jesus said He would send the Holy Spirit to be with us. It is Jesus who baptizes us in the Holy Spirit, and then as a sign of this baptism, we speak in a heavenly language. Let's ask Jesus to baptize us in the Holy Spirit.

I ask you, Jesus, to baptize me now with the Holy Spirit. I receive this infilling of Holy Spirit!

Now by faith, just speak out a sound, and let it come out of your belly, not from your head. It is okay if it is just one sound. The more you use it, the more fluent of a prayer language you will have.

There were not any Bible conferences or seminars that I could attend in my area, only my Tuesday Bible women's group. We can receive the baptism of the Holy Spirit at home alone by faith or in a group of people by faith. It is the Holy Spirit who promises to teach us Scripture and to comfort us and counsel us.

As for you, the anointing you received from him remains in you and you do not need anyone to teach you. But as his anointing teaches you about all things and as that anointing is real, not counterfeit—just as it has taught you, remain in him.

1 John 2:27, NIV

When the women at my study told me that someone was coming to our area to minister, which was seldom, I was eager to attend. A woman named Helen Velonis was scheduled to speak in a nearby town of Crookston, Minnesota. I was excited to hear her and was about to experience the impartation of gifts by the laying on of hands and this would set the course of my life.

What Kind of Love is This?

Six

Impartation Through Laying on of Hands

On November 19, 1987, I went to Crookston to hear Helen Velonis speak about her life. She was a pastor of a church in Lyle, Minnesota called Jesus is Lord. Helen was a prophet and evangelist. She shared about her life growing up in Ukraine, about experiencing war in her country and the many difficulties. Her mother died there. Helen, her sister, and her father fled to the United States in 1949 when Helen was 16 years old. She was unable to speak English, so getting a job in the United States was difficult. She began prostitution in order to have money to purchase food. This led to her use drugs and chemicals.

While in this lifestyle, she began to hear the Lord share His love for her. She gave her heart to Jesus one day and was miraculously able to read an English Bible without being taught English. She accepted the role of a pastor and moved from California to Lyle, Minnesota founding Jesus is Lord church. She told about her horrible lifestyle of drugs and prostitution and how the love of God pursued her and won her over.

I was so touched by Helen's compassionate heart. She prayed for each person one-by-one who came to hear her. When she prayed for me, I could smell a sweet fragrance of perfume on her. Assuming it was a perfume she was wearing; I didn't think anything more about it. Three significant events happened to me within the next twelve hours after this woman laid hands on me. Many years later I discovered those events would be representative of three significant seasons of my life.

When she began praying for me, I was unable to stand and was not even aware of how I ended up lying on the floor. Later in searching out scriptures for this, I found this was referred to *being slain in the Spirit*. The weight of God's glory is explained throughout scripture.

When I saw him, I fell at his feet as though dead. Then he placed his right hand on me and said: "Do not be afraid. I am the First and the Last.
Revelation 1:7, NIV

When the disciples heard this, they fell facedown to the ground, terrified.
Matthew 17:6, NIV
and the priests could not perform their service because of the cloud, for the glory of the Lord filled the temple of God.
2 Chronicles 5:14, NIV

While lying on the floor, I was in a place of looking down from the ceiling at all the people who were in the room. I didn't understand what happened that I was able to see all of this, so I didn't say anything to anyone. I knew if this was God that He would show me in His Word, and my experience would have to agree with Scripture in the Bible. This was the first event that occurred to me after this woman laid hands on me. Later, I read 1 Samuel.

God Still Heals People Today

Formerly in Israel if a man went to inquire of God, he would say,

> *Come, let us go to the seer*
> 1 Samuel 9:9, NIV

A seer is a person who "sees," and is another name for a prophet. More specifically, a seer was a prophet who saw visions or pictures or scenes seen in the mind's eye, in dreams, or even with one's natural eye. God imparts gifts to people through the laying on of hands. It may have been that I received a seer gifting from Helen who was a prophet. It may have also been a vision like in Acts 2.,

> *In the last days, God says I will pour out my Spirit on all people,*
> *Your sons and daughters will prophesy, your young men will see visions, your old men will dream dreams.*
> Acts 2:17, NIV

This is one of those things that I learned to put things on-the-shelf of my life until I could gain an understanding of its meaning for me.

The second unordinary event that occurred after hearing Helen Velonis was that night when I had a dream, which I knew without a doubt was from God. Even though I didn't know how to apply the dream to my life, it was vividly clear and imprinted upon my heart.

In this dream, I had left my home and my family at a really young age, which in real life I did. Then, after a long time of being away, I was now returning to my home. I was so excited to be returning home and to be with my family once again. I imaged hugging them and telling them how much I loved them, how much I had missed them, and how glad I was to be with them again.

In my dream I entered the home that I grew up in, but I was not greeted with the same excitement and love that I carried within me. I literally felt an unimaginable emotional pain of rejection inside of me during this dream.

I didn't understand this dream, so I put it on-the-shelf, so to speak, so God could give me the understanding of it at a later date. This dream was the second significant event I received after Helen Velonis laid hands on me.

The next morning at 6:00 am, I went to work at a nursing home where I was employed as a nurse. When I entered the first resident's room at this facility, I could smell a sweet fragrance of perfume. I recognized it as the same fragrance Helen Velonis had been wearing the night before. It caused me to stop in the doorway of my resident's room to pause and take notice of the aroma because it was so strong and beautiful.

I had showered the night before and had put on completely different clothes, so there was not anyway there could be even a trace of Helen's perfume residue on me. I realized the wonderful smell had to be a spiritual fragrance.

The fragrance of the Lord is spoken of in 2 Corinthians.

> *For we are to God the aroma of Christ among those who are being saved and those who are perishing.*
>
> 2 Corinthians 2:15, NIV

God Still Heals People Today

This supernatural fragrance was the third significant event that occurred after this woman laid hands on me and prayed for me. These three significant events all occurred within twelve hours of Helen Velonis praying for and laying hands on me.

The Bible talks about receiving impartations when laying on of hands. This is most often how gifts are imparted and transferred from one person to another in Scripture.

When Helen prayed for me that night, I received an impartation of the gifts that were on her life. These are some Scriptures that talk about impartation through the laying on of hands.

Then Peter and John placed their hands on them, and they received the Holy Spirit.

Acts 8:17, NIV

Now Joshua, son of Nun was filled with the spirit of wisdom because Moses had laid his hands on him. So, the Israelites listened to him and did what the Lord had commanded Moses.

Deuteronomy 34:9, NIV

For this reason, I remind you to fan into flame the gift of God, which is in you through the laying on of my hands.

2 Timothy 1:6, NIV

So, after they had fasted and prayed, they placed their hands on them and sent them off.

Acts 13:3, NIV

When Helen prayed for me, I was slain in the Spirit and either had a vision or a seer gift in operation. That night I had a revelatory dream that would play out in the years to come. The next morning, I carried the same fragrance of the Lord, which is a fragrance of love and compassion that Helen had on her life.

I was not concerned about understanding everything God was doing but would search the Scriptures to explain what He was doing in my life. If I didn't understand, I would set aside until He gave me the revelation and understanding.

When you have a relationship with someone, you automatically talk and spend time with them. This is what I was doing with God, having a relationship, with no set of rules or steps to take. I trusted God to talk to me and to walk with me and to help me to know Him without thinking anything more of it. In the process, I was learning to discern what was of Him and what was not of Him. We are supposed to live supernatural lives here on earth, walking by the spirit and not according to our fleshly desires. It is a supernatural type of life, but it is meant to be walked out naturally because of love and not because of a law.

Now, at my women's study, I was grasping the truth of praying for sick people to be healed. I did not grow up with this knowledge or experience, so I had become aware there was much I didn't know or understand. I was becoming aware that God's love had the ability to change many things, including people's hearts and people's physical bodies. He was not the author of sickness and disease; He was indeed the healer.

Seven

God Still Heals People Today

When I realized that Satan comes to kill, to steal, and to destroy a person's life, I gave more of my heart to the Lord. I told God that I would go anywhere He wanted me to go, I would say anything He wanted me to say, and I would do anything He wanted me to do.

The next twelve years of my life was mostly focused on caring for my three young children, working a full-time nursing position, growing in the knowledge of God through this little Bible study, and living in a difficult marriage.

I wasn't in touch with world news or current events because I did not take time to listen to television or radio. I had a hunger to know the things of God. I did not shop in stores for anything other than the necessities for me and my children. We had none of the extra things in life, just the very basics. I was somewhat isolated from society due to my unhealthy marriage relationship. Not knowing what else to do I drew closer and closer to God.

The Holy Spirit taught me how to play guitar. When I heard others sing on VHS tapes, I would write down the songs. The young women circulated these VHS tapes around our Bible study. I put my own chords to the lyrics, and these were the songs I sang to the Lord in my bedroom.
I spent my time getting to know who God was.

Outside of my nursing employment and chores at home, I spent most of my time singing songs to the Lord, studying Scripture, and talking with Him. It was fun, peaceful, and fulfilling to my soul.

The house where I attended my weekly Bible study belonged to a woman named Gladys Jacobson who was eighty years old. My children thought this was their grandmother because we went there every week. She would make homemade donuts and pastry treats for us to eat. We would sing, talk about Scripture and how it applied to our lives, then pray for one another and laugh together.

In this small home fellowship, we talked mostly about the compassion of God and how this love healed people in the New Testament. When Jesus prayed for people, He was always moved with compassion toward them. The Bible says in Hebrews 13 that God never changes.

Jesus Christ is the same yesterday, today, and forever.
Hebrews 13:8, NIV

God always has been and still is in the business of loving people and healing them. Isn't that good news! He hasn't changed! The Bible is supposed to be good news!

This Bible study was the first place I had ever heard that God heals people. I began reading all the testimonies in Matthew, Mark, Luke, and John. Having worked at a hospital and nursing home, I saw sick people every day, but I had never seen anyone healed or even heard of anybody praying for a sick person in a hospital or nursing home setting.

There came a time when I had a discussion with God about this. I had never seen anyone healed and had never seen any miracles in my lifetime. If God's word in the Bible

God Still Heals People Today

is really true, then I felt that I should be able to see this in my life.

I felt the Lord impress upon me to talk to just the sick people He directed me to talk to. I felt that when I talked to them, He wanted me to share His love with them. Having already seen what love did in my father's life and how it changed him, I was encouraged. This all seemed to be a pretty simple thing for me to do in order to bring healing to someone.

One day at work, I came to a certain woman's room. I felt God impress upon me to share His love with her. She was mentally and physically the sickest woman there. I had already been praying for her because I felt so bad for her and for her husband.

This woman couldn't talk, she would just scream out or make groaning sounds. Her face was disfigured with anguish. She couldn't walk and for our safety and hers, we had to tie restraints around her so she wouldn't fall out of bed or out of her wheelchair. She could harm us or harm herself if she wasn't securely tied with these restraints. She would physically attack the staff. This was in the 1980s when restraints were still allowed in facilities.

When I gave her medication, it would just drool out of her mouth because she wasn't able to swallow very well. I remember saying to her that these pills really weren't going to do much good anyway. I felt such compassion for her being in this horrible condition. I put my arms around her and told her that God loves her. There was no sign that she comprehended what I said, so I asked God to show this woman how much He loves her. Then I helped her lay down in her bed for the night. My shift ended, and I returned to work the next day.

The night nurse reported this woman had been awake all night, talking in her right mind while lying in bed. Previously, she was not able to talk. She could only scream and mumble words. To the night nurse, this woman appeared to be in her right mind.

The next day when I came to work, I saw her walking down the hall with a nurse by her side. She was completely normal in every way. She didn't need to have this nurse help her walk, but the nurse was not accustomed to this woman walking at all and her nursing care plan stated she should be tied in a wheelchair.

I didn't say anything to anyone because I was as shocked as everyone else was that this woman appeared normal. I didn't comprehend that God's love healed this woman the night before when I prayed for her. I had never seen anyone healed before and surely not an awesome miracle like this. God was showing us what His love looked like. Yet no one, not even me, understood what happened to her.

This was the first time I ever prayed for anyone. A mentally insane woman was completely changed and in her right mind! What amazing love God has for us. But I was about to learn a lesson. I didn't know I should explain to the woman that God healed her. I didn't know I should give her the opportunity to accept Jesus Christ as her savior. I was just learning about praying for sick people and didn't know there was more I need to do to help her.

After three days, this woman went back to her original state. I believe she could have remained healed if I had told her what had happened and helped her walk out her faith until she became stronger.

I have heard other ministers say that behind every mentally ill person is a traumatic experience. So many of us have traumatic things happen in our lives such as the death of a loved one, disappointments, divorce, loss of a job, accidents, and many other things. If we don't receive emotional and mental healing from these experiences, we can develop a weakness in our emotions and in our mental functions that can cause us to become unstable.

Everyone experiences traumatic things. God's future for us is not that we become mentally unstable. Our soul consists of our mind, our will, and our emotions. This is what makes us human. God wants us to be made whole physically, mentally, emotionally, and spiritually.

May God himself, the God of peace, sanctify you through and through. May your whole spirit, soul and body be kept blameless at the coming of our Lord Jesus Christ.
1 Thessalonians 5:23, NIV

On another certain day I went to another woman's room. She had been confined to her bed because of a fractured hip. Her hip was not calcifying, so she could not put weight on her leg; therefore, she had to remain in bed. I felt God gently nudge me to share His love for her. I didn't know what I was going to say to her, but expected as I start talking, the conversation would open up so I could pray for her.

I shared that God sees her lying in bed day after day, and that He cares about her and loves her. I asked her if I could pray for her, and she said I could. I prayed that her hip would begin to calcify and that she could get out of bed soon. That was all I prayed.

A couple days later, she was scheduled to have an xray. It revealed that her hip was 90 percent calcified. This was a complete surprise to the doctors. They also discovered that her legs had become the same length.

I was not aware that one of her legs was two inches shorter than the other. She had worn a built-up shoe most of her life. She told me later that she fell off of a horse when she was a young girl, and ever since that time, one leg was two inches shorter than the other, but now her legs were even.

I told this woman it was God who healed her hip and made her legs even. I encouraged her to tell her family and others what God had done for her. I have now seen people healed in their emotions, minds, physically, delivered of alcohol abuse and their hearts changed. Wow!

One night while I was at work, it was quiet with all the residents sleeping in their beds. I was walking down a long empty corridor. It was so peaceful, empty, and spacious that I had the overwhelming desire to do cartwheels. I took off doing one cartwheel, then two cartwheels, and then a third. That was so fun! I loved gymnastics in school, and it brought me back to that time.

Then in that spacious empty hallway, I began singing a song I had never heard before. It was a prophetic song that came from the heart of God. It went like this in an E minor chord.

God Still Heals People Today

My God is bigger than sickness.
My God is bigger than adverse circumstance.
He can heal me and my family,
He can set the people of Fertile free.

It was a beautiful little song that just bubbled out of me. I was not sick, and I did not know of any of my family members that were sick at that time.

When I got home, I wrote the song lyrics down and sat at the piano to find the chords. It was a simple little song but had so much meaning in it for me. Fertile was the name of the town I lived near, worked in, and prayed for in our little Tuesday evening Bible study.

In the years to come, I would see sickness and adverse circumstances in my life, in my family's lives, and in the people around me. God was already telling me who He was in the midst of those sicknesses and who He was in those adverse circumstances. He is bigger than all of them.

God gives us these promises to help us walk out our lives. We are to live on these promises. When we get these words or promises from the Lord, it is best to write them down lest we forget them. This was a prophetic song of the Lord. It spoke of a future time that these sicknesses and adverse circumstances would be apparent in my family and in the people around me. It was speaking now, the promise of God over those situations, which was healing.

At a church service one evening, the pastor was praying for people to be healed. I didn't have anything wrong with me that I was aware of. They were checking to see if the length of people's legs and arms were the same. As I sat in a chair and held my legs out in front of me, everyone could clearly see there was almost an inch difference in the length of my legs.

Someone shared that many times after a pregnancy, a woman's hips can get out of alignment, causing a leg to be shorter or longer than the other. So, the pastor prayed for my legs to be even. As we all watched, my shorter leg grew out to where it was even with the longer leg. This is easy to see because the feet will come into alignment with each other. We just prayed using our faith in the name of Jesus.

Then the pastor prayed for my hips to come into proper alignment. This was so exciting. How can you not love a God like this and not want to serve Him with your life? I want to love Him and know Him more each day.

If you would like prayer for healing in your emotions, your mind, or a physical healing, I would like to pray for you. God is there with you right now. Let's pray!

Father, we come to you and ask that this little one would be made whole. The blood of Jesus was shed for the forgiveness of our sins and for our complete healing. So, we appropriate the blood of Jesus for this little one's mind, will, emotions, and entire physical body. I speak to the sickness and command it to leave now. I speak to every evil spirit attached to this sickness to leave. I take authority over all traumatic events in your life and command the memory of them to be resolved in every cell of your heart, every cell in your mind and in every cell of your body and to be completely healed and restored all to a normal function. I command all pain to leave your mind, your emotions, and your physical body. I command all viruses, bacteria, and sickness to leave your body now in the power of Jesus' name. Lord, I thank you that all physical function in this person's body is restored and made every bit whole. I speak to this little one's emotions to be at peace and to come into proper balance. I speak to all mental functions to be made sound and fully in their right mind. I speak to your will and tell all compulsion and rebellion to leave. Father, I ask that your love would come into this one's heart and into this one's mind and into this one's body and restore this person to wholeness in every way. Father, I thank you so much for your great love for us. I bless your mind, will, emotions, and your whole body in Jesus' precious name. Amen!

After receiving the baptism of the Holy Spirit, I was awakened to my spiritual environment. This is not limited to certain people or just for someone who is gifted or special. The baptism of the Holy Spirit is meant for every believer in Jesus Christ to live and move and breath in. This is how we were meant to function on the earth. Because we do not know what the Bible says, or we do not have an understanding of the spirit realm, we shy away from getting answers, and that usually leads us into error or misunderstanding.

When we walk in a loving relationship with God, He promises to help us and to teach us. What we experience in the spirit realm to be "*true*" or "*of God*" should come into alignment with the Word. Experiences or encounters need to be weighed with the Word and character of God.

The Word or Scripture needs to agree with the Spirit or what the spiritual experience is. It should always lead you to Jesus and the power of His blood that paid the debt of our sins.

When we hear or see angels, this is how we will know they are angels or an evil spirit. The Holy Spirit inside of us will give us either peace or an uneasiness about a situation.

We should also find the answer in Scripture that will agree with the Holy Spirit. Being in close relationship with people, growing in the knowledge of the Lord is very important.

Eight

Angels or Another Spirit

My parents gave me a guitar for Christmas when I was sixteen. I learned to play notes on it but had difficulty knowing how to actually play it and strum on it. I had never taken lessons, but I had a sheet of notes that showed finger placement, and I learned from there. After being filled with the Holy Spirit, I desired to pick up this guitar again and try to learn to play some of our Bible study worship songs.

While spending hours almost every day playing in my bedroom, I could sense the presence of the Holy Spirit with me. He was teaching me to play guitar and worship, and in time I began playing songs at our Bible study and then at other gatherings.

Early in my relationship with the Lord, I heard a man sing a song called *Lily of the Valley* on a VHS. It resonated with me so much that I wrote the words down on paper and went to the piano to find and write out the chords. After finding the chords, I could then play it on guitar.

I sang this song over and over for several years. Before sharing this song with others, I first recorded this song so I could hear how it sounded. When I played it back, I heard someone harmonizing with me in the song. Only my children were in my bedroom with me, and the harmony was not coming from their little child voice.

My children's voices would be talking and singing in the background, and then there was this harmonizing that I could hear. It could have only come from an angel. I was shocked when I first heard this.

What Kind of Love is This?

Evidently, my children and I weren't alone in my bedroom during these times of singing. We were just having fun doing this, but it was still worship. My children would jump and dance on my bed and laugh and sing. This was all worship to the Lord. Worship is meant to be enjoyed. Heaven hears and enjoys our worship too.

The song *Lily of the Valley,* talks about walking through the night, which are the tests and trials in our lives. If we look to God for help during these times, He will show us how to live so that we can come through these nights and grow in beauty in His eyes.

We will need to forgive everyone along the way and not let any root of bitterness grow in our hearts. This is not easy to do, and we cannot keep our hearts right without God helping us.

This song talks about having His sweet aroma fill our lives. After we have gone through trials and tests and have kept our hearts pure, having no offense toward anyone, there will be a sweet-smelling fragrance that will emanate from us because it is the Spirit of God in us.

Even as the roses grow in beauty in God's eyes, so can we. We can be a reflection of His love. With this song, I was asking for God's wisdom and for Him to show me things I had never seen before. I wanted to be His witness so that His love would shine through me even in the night times.

During many years of ongoing difficulties, I didn't understand why I was going through what seemed like abnormal difficulties over such a long period of time. This song would come to my remembrance that I had sung so often, along with the angel that harmonized with me on the tape recorder.

Angels or Another Spirit

God was telling me that there would be the night season in my life, and He wanted to use that to form His compassion in me. God was telling me that He would still be standing near me in this dark season. God was saying that He can take the wrong things and make them right, but I would have to release them all to Him. God goes through the night seasons with us, and His angel's even minister to us during these times. We are not left alone, though we may feel as if we are all alone.

At one time we needed a better car, so after some discussion with my husband, we agreed that I would set out to find a car for myself. Even though I had always worked full-time, I had never purchased my own car. I was so excited and really taking ownership of this responsibility.

I would take my young daughter and travel to neighboring towns to investigate dealerships, wanting to make just the right purchase. After two months of shopping, each time sharing what I found with my husband, sorting out the information, I finally found the car that was just right for me. I didn't purchase it right away but instead went home to share my intentions with my husband. I planned to go back the next day to make my purchase.

That evening my husband came home after work driving a new car. It was a red Toyota, something I would have never bought. He said he had purchased that car. I was shocked because I had no idea, he considered buying a new car. He didn't talk with me before making the purchase. He also told me that we could not afford two car payments, so I would not be able to purchase the car I had found. I was crushed.

What Kind of Love is This?

Instead of yelling at him and just buying my own car anyway, I talked to God that night about what had happened. During that time, I noticed an unusual pain in the center of my stomach that had never been there before. When I went to bed, this pain remained in my stomach. After two days with this pain, I was still trying to grasp that my husband had bought a car without asking me when he knew I was shopping for a car and was talking with him every day about it. I continued to go to work and carry on my normal functions, but I was saddened by this event. Carrying this physical pain in the center of my stomach, I could not identify what was wrong or what was causing it.

After the third day, I got alone with God in my bedroom and asked Him what this pain in my stomach was. The pain began when I first talked to God about my husband buying his car and I didn't get to purchase the one I had picked out. I heard God tell me, "This is how I feel when my children do not talk to me before they make their decisions."

After God shared this with me, the pain immediately went away. He didn't tell me how wrong my husband was or anything about how he hurt me. God was just letting me know He felt the same way when I didn't come to Him and talk to Him when I made decisions in my life.

We create problems in our lives when we don't ask God for help, guidance, or direction. He has plans for us, and we only need to talk to Him about our choices. He promises to be with us, lead us, counsel us, and help us.

When we make certain life decisions, it can take us down a wrong road, and it may take a while to get back on a right road. This really saddens the heart of God because He has good plans for us and wants to Father us.

Angels or Another Spirit

On occasion, I would meet with a girlfriend several miles away so we could pray together for our families. One particular time I took my three-year-old son with me. After our morning prayer together, I set out to travel home. It had begun to snow. I drove several miles down the gravel road recognizing it was a little slippery. I was getting close to an intersection, where I would have to heed the stop sign. As I pressed down on the brakes of my car, they did not respond because of the ice that had formed on the gravel road.

On my right, I could see a large van quickly approaching the intersection. The van did not have a stop sign, and it was traveling very fast on the smooth pavement.

The van did not notice I was having difficulty slowing down, and they were showing no intention of slowing down either. In a flash of a moment, I quickly analyzed the situation. I knew my little car would be meeting the van in the middle of the intersection.

My son was sitting next to me in the front seat. He was sitting on his knees looking out his window on the right side toward this approaching van. I did not have him in a car seat nor was he strapped in his seat. I did not tell him to sit down. I did not tell him to quickly jump in the back seat because I knew there was not time for him to respond. I did not want to yell at him and become frantic towards him because we were already in a hopeless situation. I knew he would be hit first by the fast-moving van, and it would not make any difference where he was sitting. He would not even know what would be hitting him because he would surely be killed instantly. I was absolutely sure of this. I was also pretty sure

I would be killed. This van was large and was moving at a fast pace. I had a very small car; a Toyota.

Then I looked in front of my car, and I could vaguely see a shadowed figure of someone stretching their arms across the front of my car. Their arms reached across the front of my car from one side to the other side. My car began to slow down ever so gently. I still had my foot pumping on the brake, but I did not feel my brake grabbing a hold of the road. Yet my car was slowing down. We just barely missed the back of this van by the sliver of a hair as we passed safely through the intersection.

As I coasted safely through the intersection, I realized I was still alive. I realized my son was still alive and still looking out his window, unaware of what had just happened. I was in a state of shock. I couldn't talk. I could hardly move my body. I could hardly muster up the strength to continue driving my car. I drove home ever so slowly the next twenty miles while reevaluating what I had just witnessed in front of my car that saved our lives. I was so physically weakened by this whole ordeal and so aware of the mercy of our loving God who is a Father to us. Surely, He does watch over us.

I knew God sent an angel to the front of my car to slow it down and to save us from disaster. This is the loving God that we have. God was there to help me through what could have brought death to my son and to me. I had two other small children at home that would not have had a mom or their brother, if we would have collided with the van that day.

Many times, God uses angels to come to our aid. An angel ministered to us in our time of trouble and

Angels or Another Spirit

unavoidable disaster by slowing down our car and preventing an accident. I am sure there are many times in all of our lives that an angel has intervened, and we were not even aware of it.

In 1991, my three young children and I went to a New Year's Eve celebration at a high school gymnasium in Mahnomen, Minnesota. This event was open to all the churches in the area. We were all supposed to bring a song, scripture, word of encouragement, or whatever we wanted to share. We all came together from different faiths to sing songs and love God together in bringing in the New Year.

The pastor was up front reading scripture while walking back and forth in front of the people gathered together. My three-year-old son became excited and pulled on my arm and told me he could see an angel walking beside the pastor. Then my other son, who was four, told me he saw an angel sitting in the bleachers along the side of the room. My children had never shared anything like this before. They were looking so intently at what they were seeing. They were excited, and they described clearly to me what they saw.

Then one by one, we got to share the talent that we brought. A young man played his trumpet. Grandmother Gladys, who came with me, wrote a poem and read it. Two little girls sang a song together. I sang a song without any music about Pharaoh and all his chariots drowning in the sea, the ten plagues, and Moses delivering the Israelites. It was so fun. There was no formal agenda. We just enjoyed each other and shared what we brought.

The speaker ministered personal words of encouragement to each person. This is called prophecy. It is for edification, exhortation, and comfort.

What Kind of Love is This?

My three-year-old, Steven, had words spoken over him that, "He was a slugger and would touch many through mercy and love. He would cry in front of people and they will give their hearts to God."

My other two children received similar words. Billy, who was four years old, had a word spoken by the pastor that, "He liked to figure out how things work, had a scientific mind of much wisdom and would stand for justice."

My daughter Heather, who was seven, was told, "She was a go-getter and liked to get in there and play with the boys at school, that she would play an instrument, and God was going to bring her a few very close friends."

We all had such a wonderful time together that New Year's Eve. I traveled sixty miles in thirty-below weather with my three small children and Gladys. We didn't return home until way past midnight.

The children never became tired that night, and they never fell asleep until they got home into their beds. In northern Minnesota, this is how we lived and moved and had our being in God. It was so wonderful. It was such a fun event. Though I felt the sadness and loneliness of having to attend functions without my husband; my children and I were having experiences with God, and God was revealing Himself to us in so many ways.

One evening I went to a neighboring town for a tent meeting. I drove my car, taking another girlfriend and Gladys. Gladys always rode with me to special meetings. We sang songs and heard an encouraging word from a pastor. He then prayed for those who were sick. It was a wonderful evening.

Angels or Another Spirit

Then we proceeded to drive home. Believe it or not, but for a few moments it was quiet in our car of three women. We must have all been in deep thought about the evening we had just experienced. Then I began to hear what I thought was Gladys in the back seat of my car singing. It was one of the songs we had just sung at the tent meeting we attended. It was the most beautiful voice.

I listened to her beautiful voice for quite some time until finally, I said, "Gladys that song you are singing is so beautiful."

Gladys replied back to me, "I'm not singing. I thought that was you."

We were both quite shocked. I had to slow the car way down and turn on the dome light. We all looked around in the car and yet there were just the three of us in the car. We all came to the conclusion that we had all just heard an angel singing one of the songs from the tent meeting. Of course, that was the most exciting part of the whole evening.

It just makes one, more aware of the supernatural presence that is among us. I would really rather have God's presence around me than Satan's presence. I would much rather be seeing and hearing angels than some ugly critter from the kingdom of darkness.

Just because we live in a world that we can touch, see, smell, hear and taste doesn't mean that is all there is to experience in our world. According to scripture, the things in the spirit world are more real than the things in our physical world.

God is real, and we don't see Him. Jesus is real, but we don't see Him. Holy Spirit is real, but on a normal day, we don't see Him either. Angels are real, but again we don't normally see them. Our eyesight is not the only physical sense to experience the things of God, and we should not limit everything to what we see.

We can touch, see, smell, hear, and taste things in the natural and things in the supernatural. We just want to make sure that our experiences are being led by the Spirit of God and not by any other spirit because any other spirit would be of Satan. If we are created in God's image, we should be able to experience God with all of our five senses. We should have all of our five senses exercised to discern if it is good or evil.

That is why God wants us to have gifts of knowledge, wisdom, discernment, and all the other gifts of the Holy Spirit. These are to help us walk by the Spirit of God and to bless others. .

People often say, "I don't need that gift," or "that gift is for someone else," or "if God wanted me to have that gift, He will give it to me, so I'll just wait until He does."

Then they make no attempt to search God out or pursue the things He has for them. We desperately need the gifts God offers to us so that we can rightly discern what we are hearing, seeing, tasting, smelling and sensing. We need them so we can rightly respond to the things around us. These gifts are not medals we wear, but they are tools to live godly lives and to bless and help others with.

We are spirit, and we have a soul, which is our mind, will, and emotions, and we live in a physical body. There are angels and there are evil spirits. We live in a natural world, but there is also a supernatural world that we can experience.

Angels or Another Spirit

We need to be led by the Holy Spirit of God into spiritual things. This is why how we live our lives is important so that we don't become involved with evil things and be led by a spirit other than the Holy Spirit. These evil things can and *do* affect us.

I visited a friend at a nursing home on Christmas Eve. Upon entering her room, I had an unexpected event unfold. She was always cheery when I came to visit her, and she loved to visit with me. This particular evening as I entered her room and she wouldn't even look at me. It was as if she knew I had entered her room but her whole focus was on something else in the room. She was wide awake but focused intently on something that was on her bed. I came closer to her and sat in a chair next to her bed. She still wouldn't look at me and appeared to be really sad, motionless, and intently focused on something on her bed and on her dresser.

I knew there was something supernatural going on. I knew she didn't take any psychotropic medications that would cause her to hallucinate or be mentally incoherent. I asked her if she was all right. She said that she was all right. Then I asked her what she was looking at. She replied to me, "Well can't you see them?"

I told her, "No, I can't see what you are seeing." Then I asked her what she was seeing. She said there are little people here, and they are lying all over my bed and are all around the room.

She said they are all so sad. I told her that they should not be here because they are making her feel sad also. I asked her if it would be okay with her if I told them all to leave. She admitted that she was feeling sad having them around. She said they have all come to her at other times in her life. She agreed that it would be okay if I told them, they had to go away. I would also be telling them to never come back again.

I knew I needed her permission to tell all of them that they had to leave. If she wanted these sad spirits to stay there with her, then I would not have authority to tell them to leave.

God lets us have our way even if it is contrary to His way. If we want something that is not good for us, He is not going to come down and say we can't have that. So, if we want evil in our lives, whether we recognize it as evil or not, God will let us have it because He respects our desires.

Satan, on the other hand, will violate our wills whenever he can or whenever we allow him to. Satan will take any opportunity he can to bring sadness and sickness into our lives. Satan is the author of sickness and disease.

This woman did not have the knowledge or discernment to know these sad little people were not from God but rather from the kingdom of darkness. She didn't know she could have authority over them and could tell them all to leave her. Instead, she was becoming what they were, which was sad and depressed. This eventually would open a door in her life to more hopeless things and possibly sickness.

When I got into the room and realized that she was seeing something demonic, my first instinct was to get out of there. Of course, that would not be a good solution because then they would have power over me because I ran in fear and succumbed to them, and this woman would not be free from them either.

Angels or Another Spirit

We are to be ready in season and out of season. That means whether we feel like it or not. I didn't expect to be doing deliverance when I went to visit her, but I was nonethe-less ready.

She agreed with me that I could pray and tell them all to leave the room. I was glad that with a few words of gentle explanation to her, I was able to convince her that they were making her feel sad and that they were not good for her. So, I prayed based on a couple of scriptures in Luke.

When Jesus had called the Twelve together, he gave them power and authority to drive out all demons and to cure diseases.

Luke 9:1, NIV

I have given you authority to trample on snakes and scorpions and to overcome all the power of the enemy; nothing will harm you.

Luke 10:19, NIV

I told them that I had authority over them because of the blood of Jesus, and that they all had to leave the room, and that they had to leave this woman, and that they could not ever come back. After speaking to these demonic spirits, I asked this woman if they were all gone. She intently looked around the room. She told me there was one still sitting behind me. I felt a sick feeling inside of me when she said that, but I could not let fear enter me, jeopardizing the authority that Christ gave to me. I knew I was in the center of a conquest and needed to stand firm, not allowing any cowardice enter me. I was looking forward to this being over with. I told this last demonic spirit that it had to leave in the power of Jesus' name and could never come back.

After they were all gone, I prayed in the room and at her door for God's presence to be there. I asked God to have an angel set watch at the door so no evil could come into her room. This evil presence was causing this woman to feel sad, depressed, and hopeless. Did you know we can feel hopeless because of an evil presence?

I was learning to discern things in the spirit as I walked through life. I did not just wake up one morning and decide, "I think I will start looking for angels and demons, and see if I can tell the difference." Heavens no!

When you turn your life over to God, begin to put your trust in Him, and have a desire to search out the Bible for yourself asking God to help you, then you will begin to grow, and God will show you these things. Stay obedient to what God shows you and repent of the things He reveals to you so you can get rid of them and receive the good things He wants to give you!

One night after putting our children to bed, I went to bed and had fallen almost completely to sleep except that I was vaguely aware that my husband had just slipped into bed. Upon his slipping into bed, I saw with my spirit, and I know it was with my spirit because my real eyes were closed in sleep, an evil spirit come into the room. It was now standing at the foot of my side of the bed, staring intently at me. Still in a state of sleep, my spirit was alarmed, and I instantly feared what I saw. All of the hair on my skin was standing straight up because I was alarmed with such fear. I knew I would have to command it to leave the room, or it would overtake me in some way. I had to command it to

Angels or Another Spirit

leave, but I was so struck with fear that I was unable to speak.

Then all of a sudden, I blurted out the words, "The blood of Jesus avails for me."

When I spoke this, that evil spirit left immediately. I didn't even complete the sentence, and it left. I only got to "The blood of Jesus…" and it left so quickly, I didn't even see its legs move.

When I blurted out the words, they came out of my belly, not out of my head. I did not think from my head what I was going to speak. I spoke from my spirit.

After I loudly blurted out these words, I had jarred myself awake. I must have spoken pretty loudly, because my husband grumbled something, got out of bed, and went into the living room. I am sure he had no idea what I had seen.

I was as shocked seeing the demon as he was to hear me yell out "The blood of Jesus avails for me!"

The next day, there was much tension in our home between my husband and I. We were not fighting. It was a silent spiritual tension. I didn't know what to do with this tension I felt in our home. Then I realized it had to do with the demon I had seen the night before. I asked God what kind of demon that was. I heard Him say, "whoredom."

That was all I heard Him say. I wasn't thinking about anything, that was just what I heard, so I believe I heard God tell me exactly what it was. Realizing I had authority over it, and remembering how it quickly left the room when I commanded it to leave the night before, I decided to anoint our driveway and command the spirit of whoredom to leave our home and our land.

What Kind of Love is This?

I took some Canola oil to use for anointing oil to the end of my driveway, my three small children and a couple cats followed me. I poured the oil across our driveway and spoke to the evil spirit to leave our home and our property.

A couple days later, my husband quit his job and, without my knowledge, planned an auction sale to sell our house and belongings. He said he was going to another state to get a job and would come back to get us after he settled somewhere.

I told him I would not be leaving, and would not allow our home to be sold. A week later, there was an auction sale on our land, but I kept our home, household items and property. Then he left for another state.

This is what happens when you take authority over demons. They have to go, and they cannot come back unless you let them come back by your actions or by your words. When this demon was not allowed on our property or in our home, my husband was given a choice.

Each of us has to learn to discern things for ourselves and not depend on other people to do it for us. We discern things by finding scripture to support what we are sensing, and we can talk to God about it. We also need to hear and discern God's voice. God's voice is mostly a sweet, gentle, soft voice that comes from within us. It is not a voice that will make us rush into making a decision or push or force us in any way. It will most often be a peaceful leading that God gives us. God talks to all of us; we just need to recognize that it is Him.

One afternoon I was thinking about going to a church meeting to hear a speaker. This meeting was thirty-five miles away. I was questioning God about why I should go. I had heard this woman before, and I enjoyed her so much, but it was a long way to go, and I would be taking my three small children with me. I thought there must be some purpose for me to go. I didn't want to go to a nice meeting and then come home and have no purpose in it.

I was talking to a girlfriend on the phone about my questioning the long drive with my small kids. She suggested I pray about it for an hour and see what God said. I hung up the phone, got down on the floor, and stayed on my face for an hour talking to God.

I talked to God about all the things I had on my mind first, so I could empty that out to Him. Then I got to the real questions, which were "Should I go?" "Is there a reason why I should go to this meeting tonight?" and "God is there a purpose in it?"

I heard God reply to me that if I went to this meeting, "You can ask of Me anything that you want, and I will give it to you."

I heard it so clearly that there was no question in my heart about it. I quickly called my two girlfriends to tell them they could ask God for anything they wanted tonight, and He would give it to them. They would be going with me, and I wanted to share this with them so they could prepare themselves as to what they wanted from God.

I thought about what it was that I wanted from God. Hmm . . . I reasoned that I could ask God for a new husband, or a nice husband because that would really make sense. But those are life decisions that I can make with God's help. I wanted something else. I could have asked God for a certain amount of money to make life easier.

What Kind of Love is This?

That would make a lot of sense too. But that didn't seem right. It didn't take me very long to come up with something. I knew without a doubt that I could ask Him for whatever I wanted, and He would give it to me.

In my heart, I mostly desired the *gifts of healing* because I saw such a need for it. This gift is described in 1 Corinthians 12:9. We can all lay hands on the sick and see them healed, but the *gifts of healing* is a gift that not everyone has. I reasoned that this was something that would never run out. It would never come to an end like money, or relationships, or other things. I thought of all the people I could be a blessing to and bring restoration to their lives. This is what I really wanted.

Now about spiritual gifts, brothers, I do not want you to be ignorant . . . To another faith by the same Spirit, to another gifts of healing by that one Spirit.
1 Corinthians 12:1, 9, NIV

I took my kids, picked up my two girlfriends on the way, and we all got to the meeting that night. We sang songs while some played piano and guitar. It was so much fun. We usually sang songs at the beginning of a service. When we sang, we stood the whole time. We didn't stand up and then sit down and then stand up again. We sang all the songs for about a half hour or so, and then sat down. When we finished singing all the songs, the pastor came forward to thank the musicians, and then he said, "Now, before you all sit down, you can ask God for whatever it is that you want."

I was so shocked! I held out my hands to receive the *gifts of healing* . Then I thanked Him for it. There doesn't need to be a drum roll whenever God is going to do something major in our life. It can be so subtle that it is easily missed. God is big in the little things in life. Others at this meeting probably had no idea that they could really ask God for whatever they wanted and actually receive it. I do hope they took the pastor seriously, because God was serious.

My life had changed in so many ways when the gifts of the Holy Spirit started to flow through me with manifested results. I was beginning to see there were many hurting people, and though they did not understand the source of their sickness or difficult situation, God's love was just waiting for an invitation to come into their lives, to heal them, and to deliver them. Yet there are times that people do not recognize that God is speaking to them, and that He wants to heal them, and help them come out of difficult situations.

People end up rejecting the love of God because they don't understand who He is or because it doesn't line up with what they have been taught. They do not consider that perhaps what they were taught was wrong and is based on tradition instead of truth. When this happens, it is like missing a visitation by a really important person or friend. John says it this way.

> *He was in the world, and though the world was made through him, the world did not recognize him. He came to that which was his*
>
> *own, but his own did not receive him. Yet to all who received him, to those who believed in his name, he gave the right to become children of God—children born not of natural descent, nor of human decision or a husband's will, but born of God.*
>
> John 1:10-13, NIV

I was about to face a situation where the people didn't know the Holy Spirit. They thought they knew Him because of their tradition. God is the most gentle, kind, loving Father we could ever imagine, but there is another side of God's nature, which is a violent roaring wind and fire!

God does not just come to church on Sunday and then say "Bye, see you next week."

Nine

An Evening Bible Study at My Neighbor's House

I began attending a small church on Sundays so that my children could attend Sunday school. They announced there was going to be a special Bible study at my neighbor's home and the pastor was going to talk about Acts 1:8.

> *But you will receive power when the Holy Spirit comes on you, and you will be my witnesses in Jerusalem and in all Judea and in Samaria and to the ends of the earth.*
>
> Acts 1:8, NIV

I was so excited and hopeful they would teach on the Holy Spirit because then I could have fellowship with other people in the knowledge of the Holy Spirit. On February 23, 1990. I went to my neighbor's home to hear a muchawaited teaching on the Holy Spirit in hopes they all knew Him.

The large living room was filled with people and an overflow of people were in the kitchen. The pastor prayed and then proceeded to talk about different Bibles and different translations. He had so many Bibles that they were stacked higher than the chair he was sitting on.

One by one he told who wrote the Bible translation and why it was written in that translation. He actually ended with a conclusion that we cannot believe everything that is written in the Bible. I felt discouraged. This teaching was not going in a very good direction, nor was this what the Holy Spirit would want to say to the people.

Finally, after what seemed like over thirty minutes, he proceeded to give a teaching on the Scripture Acts 1:8. He read the verse and then told what each word meant in the verse. He identified what words were nouns and what words were verbs and how they flowed together in the Scripture. As I remember, this is what our English lessons were like in school. This pastor gave no Biblical meaning or revelation to this Scripture.

When he finished, he asked the group of quiet people in the house if they had any questions. No one said anything. I sat quietly while reasoning that if I did not say anything, then that would mean I agreed with what he was teaching. I definitely did not agree with him.

I didn't usually care to speak up in groups or make myself known, but I knew the Holy Spirit was there with us and was hearing everything that was being said. I knew that the Holy Spirit would not just sit quietly without bringing some correction to the horrible way this pastor had just presented the Bible and the Scripture Acts 1:8. Therefore, I felt compelled to formulate a reply that surely would not be in agreement with the pastor and probably not with any of the people who were there.

I did my best to explain that this Scripture was talking about the person Holy Spirit, and the word Holy Spirit is more than just a noun. I explained that receiving the Holy Spirit was how we had access to God's power in being a witness through our lives. People should be able to see a difference in us, and we should have a life in us that others

An Evening Bible Study at My Neighbor's House

did not have, which is all through the Holy Spirit. I did my best. I hadn't prepared myself to give a defense on behalf of the Holy Spirit and had never thought that I would have to give this defense. I was just hoping to make some friends.

When I finished my innocent, heartfelt explanation why I thought the pastor was wrong, there was silence. The pastor then broke the silence by saying, "Well, let's all have lunch now."

With that, the people got up and went to the kitchen. I was most shocked at the whole evening. They were speaking about Holy Spirit and didn't feel any remorse as to how they errantly talked about Him. I slipped through the kitchen around the people, thanking the woman whose home we had gathered. I excused myself, skipping the nicely prepared meal and slipping out the door. I wanted to be alone because I felt sickened regarding how the evening went. I couldn't sit and have lunch and small talk after what had just taken place and the sadness I felt inside.

As I drove my car home, I talked with the Holy Spirit. I felt so sad that they talked about Him like they did. I apologized for not having a better defense ready to give for Him, but I had done the best I could. I felt He had no disappointment in me. I can't explain in words the sadness I felt inside.

My goodness, I felt so sad to the point of crying because a person I can't even see had His feelings hurt. This person I can't even see is called God. But in the isolated and unloving world, I was living in, He was everything to me.

Driving home that late February night in Northern

What Kind of Love is This?

Minnesota, the air was frozen in stillness and several feet of white snow covered the ground. There was nothing moving outside because it was way below zero, and the only lights were in the front of my car.

At home, all was dark except for one light in the yard that revealed our house in the woods. My boots made a crisp crunching sound as I made my way across the frozen ground into a warm house.

It was quiet inside with everyone in bed. Our two little boys, ages two and three, were sleeping in the first bedroom down the hall to the left. Then on the opposite side of the hall, farther down, our seven-year-old daughter was sleeping. Then at the end of the hall was our bedroom where my husband had already gone to bed. All was quiet.

I slipped into bed still with a sad heart because the fellowship I had hoped to have with my new church was not going to be a fellowship that experienced God in the way I was discovering Him. I longed to be with people with whom I could have fellowship and grow as a Christian. It is lonely walking out Christian life and experiences by yourself, but feeling thankful for my Tuesday woman's group, I fell asleep in the frozen stillness of the night.

Then suddenly from a sound sleep, I woke up to the a noise I had never heard before, and even in hearing it, I could not identify what it was. It sounded as if a train was coming right toward our house. It was coming from the far south end of our house and sounded as if it was quickly going to make its way through the house. Living in the Midwest, I had never heard a real hurricane before, but I reasoned that this must be what a hurricane sounds like. I

An Evening Bible Study at My Neighbor's House

knew whatever it was, it was coming straight to our house and to our bedroom.

I was a little frightened because, by the violent sound of whatever this was. I knew without a doubt we were all going to take off somewhere or be splattered into pieces when this violent wind reached us. I folded my right arm upward as if I were locking my husband's arm in mine, reasoning wherever I was going, he was going to come with me.

Then in an instant, it hit our room. When it hit our room, it immediately filled every bit of space in the room. It was the brightest of lights that anyone could ever possibly see. My eyes were shut because the light was so bright, I could not look at it. I did try to open one eye, but it was so bright it hurt my eye to look at it.

There was such a centrifugal force in our room from this violent wind that my head felt it was being smashed into the mattress of the bed. It was the force of a mighty, violent type of wind. I don't know if I couldn't open my eyes because the light was so bright or if it was because the force of the wind was so strong that it held them shut. I don't know how long it was in our bedroom. It seemed like maybe thirty to sixty seconds. Then it was just gone.

I slowly opened my eyes, and the darkness and stillness of the night had returned to our room as before. There was no more noise. There was no more light. My right arm was still bent with my right hand next to my right ear.

With my left hand, I slowly brought my right arm back down to my side. It was painful to move my right arm, so I had to go slowly to move it downward. It had been locked so tight in the upward position that it felt like the blood flow had been cut off. The wind was so violently strong that my body felt like it had been embedded into my bed, and it was difficult to correct my body's physical position.

I very slowly turned my head to the left to look at my clock. It was 4:00 am. Lying there in the now complete silence, I didn't have any idea what just happened, but I knew I would have to find a Scripture on it in order to discern if it was God or not.

In my bed, I laid in wonderment, not even considering getting up to check on our children because I didn't know if I could get up and out of bed or physically walk. I wondered how I would explain this to anyone.

Ten

Better Put This on the Shelf

When I woke up in the morning, I went to the kitchen to prepare some breakfast and collect my thoughts. My husband had already left the house for work and didn't wake me to discuss anything unusual during the night. We didn't discuss anything about the Bible study I attended the evening before.

He had told me years earlier that he didn't want to hear anything about God, so I didn't ever say anything to him. I had asked him to come to church with me several times, but he wouldn't. He didn't come to any of our children's programs either, so when he said he didn't want to hear anything from me about God, I didn't say anything. I prayed and fasted often for his heart to be softened. I attempted to walk in love and kindness towards him, leaving it up to God to change his heart.

As our children woke up and came to the kitchen, for breakfast, I asked them if they heard anything during the night. To this day, I am not sure exactly what they said, but they all expressed in their own way that they heard something.

At their young age, they may not have been very familiar with a train or knew what a tornado was. I don't think they knew how to describe what they heard, if they indeed heard anything or saw anything at all like I did. I can't remember how they described what they experienced, but they seemed to identify with something happening.

If someone had asked me what I heard or saw during the night, I might have also hesitated about how to answer them. I heard a strong wind, and I saw a very bright light. Had I shared this with my neighbors or friends, I might have been committed for some kind of a psychological evaluation!

I mentioned this experience to one of my close friends from our Tuesday evening Bible group. I really was questioning if it had something to do with the Holy Spirit, after all, it had been our topic of discussion the evening before. I was hoping to find someone with an open mind, with whom I could share my experience. Since I never drank alcohol or took drugs, I anticipated my experiences held some validity.

My friend listened to me as I tried to explain to her what happened in our home at 4:00 am. My friend looked me straight in the eye and questioned if I had lost my mind. There was not much discussion about it. I thought if I ever experience things like this again, I probably will need to just ask God about it.

I knew it sounded kind of far out there, yet I knew what I heard, and I knew what I saw. I was there. I understand where my friend was coming from, and I understood her response. I might respond the same way if someone else had this experience and told me about it.

After I was baptized in the Holy Spirit in 1982, I had an increase in spiritual experiences, saw angels on several occasions, and saw evil spirits. I was not seeking to have any of these experiences, just reading my Bible and attending a study every week.

One of the women at this home Bible study had a satellite and would tape teachings from Trinity Broadcasting Network with Paul and Jan Crouch. We would circulate

Better Put This on the Shelf

these teachings. We also had a pastor and his wife from Crookston, Minnesota who occasionally oversaw our group and would share with us. Later we had a pastor from Neillsville, Minnesota come once in a while to oversee our group and share with us.

I desired to read my Bible so I could understand what was in it, and I was praying so I could learn to hear and know God's voice. In 1 Corinthians 12 it talks about spiritual gifts. Nine gifts are listed there. The gifts include the word of wisdom, the word of knowledge, faith, the gifts of healing, working of miracles, prophecy, discerning of spirits, different kinds of tongues, and interpretation of tongues.

Discerning of spirits is the ability to distinguish whether a source of what is being presented is of divine, human or of demonic origin. These gifts are all outworkings of the Holy Spirit. If the Holy Spirit reveals something to you, He has a purpose for it. It can help you pray more effectively or work alongside the Holy Spirit. I was not seeking to have any spiritual experiences. I only wanted to know God and love Him.

When I didn't understand the experience of the strong wind and bright light in our house that February night, I put it on the shelf, until I could search it out and hear from God what it was. I depended upon the Lord to show me in the Word where it was and give me an understanding of it.

After visiting with one friend about this experience, I didn't ask any of the other women in my Bible study what they might have thought.

Eleven

It Was the Holy Spirit

I asked God to show me an example in the Bible of the experience I had in my bedroom. I know I was thinking way too hard because I was trying to find a story in the Old Testament that would relate to this experience. I hadn't yet realized the most evident answer was Acts 1:8.

Maybe I was traumatized, but I just couldn't find a Scripture to validate my experience. Then I read in the Old Testament that the priest couldn't stand when he went into the Holy of Holies.

The priest could not enter the temple of the Lord because the glory of the Lord filled it.
2 Chronicles 7:2, NIV

In this Scripture, the glory of the Lord was in the temple so strongly that the priest could not enter, but it didn't say anything about there being a wind or a burning bright light. I continued to search for a scripture or story that would explain my experience. This is how you test spiritual things.

Scripture tells us to test every spirit to know whether it is from God or not.

What Kind of Love is This?

Dear friends, do not believe every spirit, but test the spirits to see whether they are from God because many false prophets have gone out
into the world,

1 John 4:1, NIV

Test everything, hold on to the good.
1 Thessalonians 5:31, NIV

One day I was in my kitchen cooking, and my children were playing in the house. I had a small television on the counter and was playing a DVD that we circulated with each other from our women's group. This particular day, I was listening to Benny Hinn. He was teaching on Acts 2:2. I heard him read this Scripture.

Suddenly a sound like the blowing of a violent wind came from heaven and filled the whole house where they were sitting.

Acts 2:2, NIV

Well, that really caught my attention. I came in closer to focus on my little television. Benny Hinn continued reading.

They saw what seemed to be tongues of fire that separated and came to rest on each of them. All of them were filled with the Holy Spirit and began to speak in other tongues as the Spirit enabled them.

Acts 2:3-4, NIV

Oh, my gosh! That is the Scripture that explains what happened that early morning on February 24th, 1990, at 4:00 in the morning. It was the Holy Spirit!

I remembered the evening before, I had spoken up for Holy Spirit. I had defended Him. I had disagreed with the teaching this pastor presented and was the only one to speak up of all the people who were at that house. I couldn't help but think the Holy Spirit was pleased and even excited by my response. Could the Holy Spirit have visited us because I was not ashamed of Him? I don't really know,

It Was the Holy Spirit

but Benny Hinn's teaching was confirming what I had experienced.

I could have come to the immediate conclusion that this experience was the Holy Spirit manifesting Himself in the rushing mighty wind and the fiery bright light that night, and that it had something to do with the Bible study at my neighbor's home the night before, but then I would be relying on my own knowledge to sort this out and come to my own conclusion.

When I put this experience on the shelf, and asked God to show me if this was Him or of another spirit, He answered through another teacher. I didn't want to be deceived. So, it was okay that I didn't just accept my own experience and draw on my own knowledge. I waited for God to help me understand this.

I never talked to my husband about the evening Bible study at our neighbor's home. He told me several years before that he didn't want to hear anything about God. He didn't go to church with us nor was he very supportive of me going to the woman's study.

I didn't talk to him about the experience with the wind and the blinding, bright light in our bedroom. It didn't even go well sharing it with my Bible study friends, so I didn't think it would go well with my heathen husband either. He never asked me about it, so I assumed he slept through it all. I don't know how anyone could sleep through that, but he didn't say anything, so I guessed it was possible. All this was enough for me to sort out by myself anyway. Since I had come to know God and walk with Him, my life had not been dull!

I never did speak about this again to anyone. I didn't know what it meant to me or what I was supposed to do with this experience anyway. God has a purpose in all that He does, but until I had more understanding, I didn't know what to do with it.

Many difficult things would transpire in my life ahead, and it would not be until the summer of 2012, that I would bring this up to God again or ask Him about the meaning of it.

Twelve

"This is That, That is This"

In the summer of 2012, while I was mowing my lawn, I reminisced about my past twenty-two years. During those twenty-two years, I had moved away from my precious women's Bible study and was divorced in 1996.

For the next six years, I had found myself in court with my ex-husband eleven times, mostly centered on setting safe boundaries for myself. My family was unaware of most of these difficulties because I didn't share it with them. My parents were elderly, and I was helping them whenever I could.

With financial obligations in a single parent home, I became very busy working two and sometimes three jobs. I had gone back to college to attempt to increase my income while still working full-time, caring for my parents as able, and trying to be a parent to my children.

During this time, my youngest son became involved with drugs at the age of fourteen. He was admitted to Northland Recovery Center in Grand Rapids, Minnesota and later because of a felony, went to Thistle Dew Treatment center in Togo, Minnesota. When he was eighteen, he did not survive an overdose. My other two children were going to college and trying to establish their lives.

From 2005 to 2008, five of my family members passed away, four of them unexpectedly. During that time, my focus was on keeping a place to live, having food in our refrigerator, and taking care of other people. Dating was not anything I had time for nor any interest in. Now, in the summer of 2012, I was alone at home reflecting on my life.

While mowing lawn, I asked God why I was so unsupported emotionally during these years of trying to raise my children alone. Perhaps that is how all single parents feel, but it seemed my life was a little more difficult than the normal life, if there is a normal life.

I felt shame and even guilt about the disappointing way things had turned out. I felt I had terribly failed my children in being a good mother to them. My expectations had fallen so far below my dreams.

God reminded me of a dream I had in 1984. In the dream, I had left home at a young age, and was gone for a long time. During this time, I missed my family very much. A day came that I was able to return home. I was overjoyed and so happy to come back home. But some things had changed, and I was not received with the same joy. Instead, I felt emotionally rejected and abandoned.

That summer day in June of 2012 while mowing my lawn, I asked God why I had such difficulty after moving back to my home area. God told me "This was that." I instantly understood.

He said "this," the difficult time that I lived through for so many years, was "that," the dream He gave me in 1984. I felt a sense of relief in understanding this from Him. God let me know He had already shown me in a dream, or warned me, that it would be a difficult season of my life.

Sometimes God lets us know things in advance to warn us or to help us walk through those things. Sometimes

"This is That, That is This"

they are warnings not to go a certain way, and other times they are just informative to help us maneuver through a difficult situation. I didn't understand that dream when I had it so many years ago, but now I understood the significance of it.

These difficult times are also times of testing for us. God does not test us, but life does. It is how we respond to these difficulties that make us who we are. God will use these tests and trials to make us more like Him in our nature and character if we pass them.

When we take tests in school, we have to take them alone. No one is there to help us. Sometimes in real life, it isn't any different. This time of testing is a time that we can become bitter and angry towards other people, or we can die to our own flesh, forgive those who hurt us, and choose to still love people in spite of what they do or say.

In suffering, we are given the opportunity to forgive and learn to love. If we don't forgive and learn to love, we will die in the wilderness we are in. James 1:2-4 says it this way.

> *Consider it pure joy, my brothers, whenever you face trials of many kinds, because you know that the testing of your faith develops*
> *perseverance. Perseverance must finish its work so that you may be mature and complete, not lacking anything.*
>
> James 1:2-4, NIV

Receiving understanding about that question gave me satisfaction, so I felt I needed to ask God another question that had been on my mind for many years. I wanted to keep our conversation going.

I asked God the purpose of the Holy Spirit visiting our home in such a powerful way in February of 1990. I didn't think the Holy Spirit just visits people's homes because they defend Him at Bible studies. I thought surely God had a purpose in that wind and fire visitation. I also didn't think the purpose of this extraordinary visitation had to do with just me because the event was so much bigger than me.

I heard God answer me, "That is this." I understood what He meant in those few words.

I understood God to mean "that," which was the wind and fire visitation in 1990, is "this," which was what God planned to do next.

The visitation of the Holy Spirit that we experienced in our home in 1990 was a taste of what God is planning to do on earth in the coming move of the Holy Spirit.

The wind was so strong that the centrifugal force would flatten anything in its way. The noise was as if a freight train was going full speed ahead through the house. It was a light so bright that it would blind someone who looked at it. It was the presence of God, so powerful that no one could control it. That is what is coming.

It will be like a fire that will consume everything that is chaff within us. Anything that is not of God will be consumed. It will burn as a consuming fire everything that is not of God and will cause people's hearts to be changed. There will be a deep, repentance in people's hearts, and it will cause instant deliverance and healings to occur in people's lives; physically, emotionally, mentally, and in

"This is That, That is This"

every way. It will create such a culture shift in the way we live life that church as we know it will never be the same.

Later that June of 2012, in a rare occurrence, I took the opportunity to speak to my ex-spouse to ask him for the first time ever, if he had heard anything or saw anything that night so many years ago. Before this moment I had never brought up to him the wind and fire visitation that I believed was of God.

I only began to describe the event to him, asking if he remembered "one particular night twenty-two years ago," and he immediately knew what I was talking about.

He replied, "Yes, that was the brightest light I had ever seen!"

He went on to say that he couldn't look at it because it was so bright. He also said that he thought about it the next morning and knew it was not a dream. He knew it had happened, but he had no explanation for it. And we never talked about it until twenty-two years later when I felt prompted to ask him.

Later that same month of June in 2012, I also visited with my daughter, who was now twenty-nine years old. I was somewhat surprised at her father's response and was anxious to hear what she had to say, if anything at all.

I only briefly began to explain this event to her by asking if she "remembered anything a long time ago on a February night while we were living in Fertile, Minnesota" and she immediately knew what I was talking about.

She said, "Yes!"

Continuing, she said a loud noise woke her up during the night. She got out of bed to look down the hall, but by the time she got to her doorway to look into the hallway, the noise was gone. My daughter was seven years old at the time. This was one night, twenty-two years ago, and she remembered this one night like it was yesterday without having discussed it for all those years.

One of them testified of the blinding bright light and the other one testified of the strong wind. I was glad I had asked them because things are established when there are two or three witnesses.

> *This will be my third visit to you. 'Every matter must be established by the testimony of two or three witnesses.*
>
> 2 Corinthians 13:1. NIV

Life became busy and confusing for a long time, and our family never discussed this visitation of the Holy Spirit, but in time God confirmed it.

Thirteen

What Does This Mean? What Must We Do?

Many of us believe in God and that God created man and everything on the earth. Many believe that Jesus Christ is God's son and have heard a message on being born again or being saved through believing in Jesus Christ as our savior.

The purpose of Jesus' coming to earth as a man was to pay the debt for our sins and to be our savior. He restored our relationship with God, our Father.

When Jesus went to Heaven, He said that He was not going to leave us alone on earth. He said the Holy Spirit would be with us. Jesus came to earth as a man even though He was the son of God. It should be no more difficult for us to believe the Holy Spirit is a person and exists here with us today.

The triune God is three in one. I know that this is a mystery to understand. God the Father, Jesus the Son of God and God the Holy Spirit exist distinctly and as one. Let's see what scripture has to say.

Therefore, go and make disciples of all nations, baptizing them in the name of the Father and of the Son and of the Holy Spirit,

What Kind of Love is This?

>   Matthew 29:19, NIV

And I will ask the Father, and he will give you another Counselor to be with you forever, the Spirit of truth. The world cannot accept him because it neither sees him nor knows him. But you know him for he lives with you and will be in you.
>   John 14:16-17, NIV

Jesus is at the right hand of the Father in Heaven. The Holy Spirit is here with us to comfort us, to guide us, to counsel us, to fill us, to teach us, and to be our helper. He is those rivers of living water that come out of our belly.

On the last day and greatest day of the Feast, Jesus stood and said in a loud voice, "If anyone is thirsty, let him come to me and drink.
Whoever believes in me as the Scripture has said, streams of living water will flow from within him.
>   John 7:37-38, NIV

Holy Spirit is the breath that breathes from us when we speak the Word of God. He is the mighty sound from heaven as a hurricane wind. He is the bright light of tongues of fire. He is the suddenly sound that comes from Heaven.

In Acts 2:12, they were all amazed when the Holy Spirit came upon the 120 people in the upper room. The people in Jerusalem were asking one another the question, "What does this mean?" Peter explains what all this noise meant.

Now, this is what was spoken by the prophet Joel. "In the last days,

God says, I will pour out my Spirit on all people. Your sons and daughters will prophesy, your young men will see visions, your old men will dream dreams. Even on my servants, both men and women, I will pour out my Spirit in those days, and they will prophesy. I will

What Does This Mean? What Must We Do?

show wonders in the heaven above and signs on the earth below, blood and fire and billows of smoke. The sun will be turned to darkness
and the moon to blood before the coming of the great and glorious day of the Lord. And everyone who calls on the name of the Lord will be saved.

Acts 2:16-21, NIV

The people's hearts were pricked or their conscience smitten when they heard this. Smitten means to be overwhelmed or struck by something, usually by love. It also means to be infatuated or enamored by love.

Because of this, they were asking the question, "What shall we do?" Peter answers the crowd.

Repent, and be baptized every one of you, in the name of Jesus Christ for the forgiveness of your sins. And you will receive the gift of the Holy Spirit.

Acts 3:28, NIV

The answer is to repent and be baptized for the remission of your sins, then you can receive the gift of the Holy Spirit. This promise is for all people. God is not upset

What Kind of Love is This?

with any of us, and He really wants us to have different thoughts about Him and His purpose for our lives. He leaves the Holy Spirit with us to dwell in us and bring us comfort and counsel.

Fourteen

Something Big is Coming

On a dark evening around 6:30 pm on December 5, 2012, I was driving to my Bible study in Fargo, North Dakota. As I drove, I saw in my mind's eye an open vision of a theatre with a large deep red, velvet curtain drawn closed. Although, I sensed this curtain was going to open really soon. Then I saw behind the curtain, and it was the gathering place for our Bible study. It was quiet, no one was there. There were garments of clothing laying all around the floor and on top of chairs.

These garments had been discarded by the owners because they didn't think they would need them anymore. The people had become discouraged and thought God had deserted them, so they put down many of the things that God had previously given to them. These things were gifts and callings God had put inside of them, but because they became disappointed or lost their way, they discarded these garments. This clothing was laying all around in this room behind the red velvet curtain.

I felt God saying to His children to pick up those garments and get ready for the next Act. God was ready to turn on the floodlights of His glory. It was as if we were getting ready for a production behind this theatrical curtain.

I could tell there was a great sense of excitement going on in Heaven at this time; with lots of noise, laughter, joy, and preparations in Heaven because of what God was planning to do here on earth with His sons and daughters.

Some of the garments represented the testimonies that people had never told others that needed to be heard. Other garments were love and hope. God has a role for everyone to play in His production! He loves us and wants to include all of us in on His plans in the earth!

I believe we will see Isaiah 61 fulfilled. The brokenhearted will be healed. Divine reversal will happen to believers and unbelievers. It is the reversal switch of the *instead of's*. For our ashes, God wants to instead give us beauty. For our mourning, God wants to instead pour an oil of joy on us. For the spirit of heaviness that has oppressed us, God wants to instead remove all those controls over us and give us a garment of praise, of thankfulness, and a lightness in our spirit.

Jesus' mission in coming to earth was to heal and bind up the broken-hearted. Broken hearted people are grieving people because loss and despair has overtaken their hearts. God wants to fill us with hope and make us every bit whole, spirit, soul, and body.

For the shame we have felt, we will receive a double reward from heaven. For the confusion we have been in, God wants to give us a clear sound mind and meet all our needs. God, through the Holy Spirit, wants to pour out an everlasting joy in our lives.

> *Instead of their shame my people will receive a double portion, and instead of disgrace they will rejoice in their inheritance, and so they will inherit a double portion in their land, and everlasting joy will be theirs.*
> Isaiah 61:7, NIV

On December 10, 2013, at 2:00 am, I got out of bed and went to look out my kitchen window. It was in the middle of winter in Northern Minnesota. Several feet of snow covered the Red River Valley. It was, of course, way below zero outside.

No lights were on in my house, and no lights were on outside except for the moon. I looked out my kitchen window to the north. The sky was dark, and the ray from the moon lit up the snow-covered valley. It was a beautiful sight, full of peace.

I heard within me a gentle voice say, "There is something big coming."

I understood that the snow-covered, frozen, peaceful scene I was looking at would be the complete opposite of the "Something big that was coming" that I heard whispered in my heart.

I understood this to be so big that it would change the way we do life. I had absolutely no sense of fear when I heard these words. It gave me a sense of anticipation and expectation. I had no preconceived thoughts in my head as I looked out my dark, frozen winter window. I just got out of bed and looked out my window, and I heard the Holy Spirit's gentle voice in my heart with complete peace attached to His words.

God is saying several things to us in this coming move of the Holy Spirit and in the words of "There is something big coming."

1. All the abnormal difficulties and opposition we have experienced was a wilderness season. God will use the wilderness season to test our hearts and to prove us. It will cause us to make decisions

whether or not we will be faithful to Him and still love Him in spite of our circumstances. God uses those times to form Christ's character in us.
2. God is completely healing whole households of emotional and mental wounding. God is healing each person and their whole household of all manner of physical sickness and of all manner of disease.

3. God is going to visit homes and whole households will be affected. The babies, the children, the teens, the parents, the grandparents, great-grandparents, and the nannies. All of the households will be touched by this move of God, from sea to shining sea.

4. You won't miss it, but many may not understand it. When it comes it will wake you up. There is nothing passive about a loving God.

5. Prepare your heart for this. God will remove everything from you that is not of Him if you allow Him to. His purifying wind will blow, and His baptism of fire and love will burn everything that remains in you and in your whole household that is not of Him. This is a *purifying baptism* of wind and fire and unimaginable love that heals and restores all the broken places of your life. You will not ever be the same!

6. People will be awakened out of their sleep. They will come out of their rooms and out of their houses to see what the noise is all about. They will

Something Big is Coming

see God's fire, a spiritual type of fire, on top of homes
and other buildings where God is moving. They will instantly repent and want to know who God is.

7. You will not be able to explain what has happened to you and your household. There will not be words to identify what has happened. It is just the goodness and kindness of a loving God.

8. There will be those who will criticize and not want to believe what God is doing. They will not believe this can be of God. We need to be led by the Holy Spirit and by the Word of God because the two agree.

9. Your whole household being touched by the extravagant goodness of God. This is Acts 2:17.

This was spoken by the prophet Joel; I will pour out of my Spirit upon all people. Your sons and your daughters will prophesy, your young men will see visions and your old men shall dream dreams. Even on my servants, both men and
women, I will pour out my Spirit in those days and they will prophesy. I will show wonders in the heaven above and signs on the earth below, blood and fire and billows of smoke.

Acts 2:17, NIV

10. Take time to rest in the Lord's presence and wait on Him. No matter how busy your life is, take time to pull aside and rest with your Father, God. This is

> where your intimacy and relationship with God is forged. This is where you hear the secret things from Him. This is where your soul is restored.

In 1983 when Helen Velonis prayed and laid hands on me, I had three experiences within the next twelve hours. It would be many years later that I would understand that these three experiences were symbolic of three seasons of my life.

The first experience of being slain in the spirit, or lying on the floor after the laying on of hands, and having an open vision represented the season of my life from the time I was born again in 1976 until 1991 when I left the area of Fertile, Minnesota where my precious lady's Bible study was. It was a time of growing in the things of God and developing my relationship with Him.

The second experience of the dream in the night, which was so shocking and horrible, represented the season of my life from 1991 until 2012. This period was filled with tests and trials, sufferings and difficulties. When many things seemed to work against me, God wanted to know if I would still love Him and walk upright and according to his Word. He wanted to know if I would choose to live as the world does or if I really wanted to live according to His ways. He wanted to know if I would forgive others and if I would obey Him even when my heart was crushed and broken.

The third experience of smelling the beautiful, sweet flower fragrance while at my workplace represents the season that began in 2012 when I received a prophetic word from a prophet, causing me to inquire of the Lord where I could go to follow His purposes for my life.

I felt led to relocate to Christian International in Santa Rosa Beach, Florida where I attended their college while working as a nurse. I believe at this time I entered the third season of my life of experiencing the healing of my heart and my soul. I experienced the compassion and the love of God in this place that brought a restoration to my life. I believe the next long season of my life will be full of the goodness and grace of God as I continue to yield to Him.

God is good all the time, and He knows who you are and where you are. Ask Him what His plans are for your life. According to Jeremiah, God has good plans for you. You are here for a reason. Your life has a purpose only you can fulfill.

For I know the plans I have for you, declares the Lord, plans to prosper you and not to harm you, plans to give you hope and a future.

Jeremiah 29:11, NIV

What Kind of Love is This?

Fifteen

Peace I Leave with You

We must have our hearts right before God. If you can't identify exactly when you asked Jesus Christ into your life, you can invite Him in today. God is a gentleman who will not come in unless you invite Him.

If you would like to have this loving relationship with Jesus Christ, I would like to pray with you now.

Father, I believe that Jesus Christ is Your son, that He came to earth as a man and died for all of my sins. I believe He went to hell for me and paid my debt of sin. I believe after three days He rose from the dead and is now in heaven at Your right side.
I am sorry for my sins. I want Jesus Christ to come into my life and to wash me clean with His blood. I accept You as my Father God and I will love You all of my days. Thank You for taking me as Your son, as Your daughter. Thank You, Jesus, for eternal life.

After believing in and receiving Jesus Christ, we are to be baptized by full immersion.

Whoever believes and is baptized will be saved, but whoever does not believe will be condemned.

Mark 16:16, NIV

Ask your pastor to do this, or if he doesn't do full immersions, find a church that does. It represents dying to your old life and leaving it behind to live a new life in Christ.

We are saved by believing in Jesus Christ and have eternal life, but we are instructed to be baptized as a symbolic act of dying to our old nature with Christ unto a new and resurrected life.

After receiving Jesus Christ as our savior, we are to receive the baptism of the Holy Spirit.

I baptize you with water for repentance. But after me comes one who is more powerful than I, whose sandals I am not worthy to carry. He will baptize you with the Holy Spirit and fire.

Matthew 3:11, NIV

When Jesus went to heaven to be with Father God, He said if He didn't go, the Comforter could not come. So, it was better for Him to go. God does not leave us alone.

Nevertheless, I tell you the truth, it is to your advantage that I go away, for if I do not go away, the Helper will not come to you. But
if I go, I will send him to you

John 16:7, NIV

Jesus baptizes us with the Holy Spirit. The new language of tongues that you receive is just a manifestation that you have been baptized with the Holy Spirit.

If you would like to be baptized with the Holy Spirit, I would like to pray with you. May I reach out to you and hold your hands while we pray together?

I'll pray, and you receive the Holy Spirit.

Lord Jesus, I ask that You would baptize this one with the Holy Spirit.

Now, don't say anything in English. By faith, open your mouth and begin to utter sounds from your lips. Let the Holy Spirit speak through you. It can be just a sound. Keep releasing that sound. Allow the Holy Spirit to fill you.

The more you allow the Holy Spirit to speak to you, the more your heavenly language will grow.

Read the book of Acts to help gain understanding of the baptism of the Holy Spirit. If you still need more help, find someone to pray with you from a church that demonstrates the gifts and manifestations of the Holy Spirit. If you have any unforgiveness or any offenses, talk to God about it, and remove them from your life by forgiving those who have wronged you.

Unforgiveness may prevent you from receiving a healing in your body because many times it is the cause of sickness. If you need healing in your body, soul, or spirit, I would like to pray for you now. Healing is part of your inheritance when you become a child of God.

Heavenly Father, You said that if I don't forgive others, then You will not forgive me, in Mark 11:26: "But if you do not forgive, neither will your Father which is in heaven forgive you your trespasses." I choose to forgive this person who hurt me, who caused me pain, and who caused me hardship. I release them to You, Father. I ask You, Father, to remove the arrows of pain that shot into my heart, causing me hurt inside. I release to You my bitterness, my anger, and all my frustration that came to me during this difficult time. Remove all the infection that it has caused in my heart and in my body. (Take a moment and let Him do this for you.)

Now, Father, I ask You to pour Your balm of Gilead over me and into me, so my heart can be healed, so my emotions can be healed, and so my body can be healed. Father, I ask that You would restore my joy and my peace. I ask that You would bring to my life enriching friendships. Give me wisdom and discernment in how to live my life with peace in my heart.

Now let's pray for our families and our homes.

Heavenly Father, You are a family God. You are all about relationships and family. You created us to live with You and with each other as a family. Father, I ask that You visit every home in my family and remove everything that is not of You. Wake us up. Revive each family member with Your love. Restore our bodies, our minds, our emotions, our creative abilities, and our talents that You gave us to use on earth for Your purposes. Change our hard hearts into hearts of flesh that love You and that love one another. Have Your way in us and in our homes. Set fathers in our homes who will love and protect their families. Deliver men and women of abuses they have suffered and from a deteriorated society. May our children live in hope-filled homes that love one another. Come baptize us and purify

Peace I Leave with You

us with Your wind and fire. We invite You into our lives and into our homes to be our Lord. We need You Lord God.

In John 14:27, Jesus said He was going away to be with His Father, but the Father would send us another Comforter, who was called the Holy Spirit. One of the last things Jesus said was for us not to be afraid or troubled, and then He said He was leaving us His peace.

Peace, I leave with you, my peace I give to you. I do not give to you as the world gives. Do not let your hearts be troubled and do not be afraid.

John 14:27, NIV.

This peace is available to us as a son or daughter of God. When you belong to the family of God, peace is one of your benefits. Let's receive everything our heavenly Father has for us, and live life abundantly

What Kind of Love is This?

Endnotes

1. Wright, H. W. (2007). Insights into Addiction. Be in Health.
2. Ibid.

What Kind of Love is This?

More from the Author

A Baptism of Fiery Love is Coming

The Holy Spirit is at work in every person's life wooing and pursuing them to return to a loving relationship with Father God their Creator. This an individual process walked out by each person.

The Holy Spirit wants to introduce himself to each one of us. He came to heal our hearts and our bodies that we may have an abundant life and share in His glory. This is the beginning of an era of seeing and experiencing God's glory.

Five Smooth Stones to Slay Intimidation

God does not send us into battle without weapons. He has given us five smooth stones just like He gave to David to use against Goliath, the voice of intimidation that wants to rise up in our lives. We do not ever have to be intimidated or shut down again. Know your identity and authority God has given you. Walk in the love and grace from God that causes us to overcome all

What Kind of Love is This?

obstacles. Secure your smooth stone of humility that says, "I trust you Lord." With these five smooth stones in your sling of faith, you will slay the voice of intimidation in your life.

Revealing God's Truth on Abortion

A Study Guide for God, *What is My Baby's Name?*

"Whether you are a woman who has suffered in silence over a past abortion, a family member or friend with a loved one who has had an abortion, or a pastor or counselor, this book will provide insight, strategy and a practical process to help restore hope and wholeness to broken lives."

Jane Hamon

God, What is My Baby's Name?

Jesus came to heal the brokenhearted. The brokenhearted are those who have suffered pain in their hearts. The brokenhearted are those who are grieving over a loss in their lives and have little hope. Because of the shame and guilt a woman and man

experience when there is an abortion, they grieve in silence. There is nowhere
to go to have this pain removed. The medical field can perform all kinds of marvelous things for our bodies, but there is only one that can heal the pain of a broken heart.

Stop Steven, Stop

The trauma of losing a son to a chemical overdose hurled Susan into a grief that caused a brokenness of heart that was not able to find relief. Wholeness seemed impossible to obtain. While seeking her own healing, Susan not only obtained the healing of her broken-hearted condition but also leads the way for others who are
brokenhearted to be made whole.

Restoring Your Heart

Susan Pender shares revelation that she received from God in a dream indicating wounds that needed to mend to restore her heart and soul. She relates her personal experience to the story of Nehemiah who was moved with compassion to assist the people to repair and rebuild the city walls and gates of Jerusalem.

Susan shares how the Holy Spirit moved with compassion in her life to bring restoration to the shattered fragments of her heart and soul.

When someone is wounded by physical, emotional, or sexual traumatic events, part of their heart and soul can separate from their whole personhood. These separated parts will hold the painful emotions associated with the traumatic memory. The more someone's heart and soul are harmed in this way, the more they become literally broken within.

We may not even be aware of the painful memory that caused the trauma, but the Holy Spirit knows everything about us and can help us bring restoration to our hearts and souls and wholeness to our lives. God sent His Son Jesus to earth to die for us and the Holy Spirit to help and comfort us to restore our hearts.

God uses the metaphor of a city to describe us.

The LORD is building up Jerusalem; He is gathering [together] the exiles of Israel. He heals the brokenhearted, And binds up their wounds [healing their pain and comforting their sorrow].

Psalm 147:2, 3, AMP

The ruins and desolate places reveal areas that are broken within you. The exiles are all the broken pieces of your heart and soul that need to be healed and integrated back into their rightful places within you to make you whole again. God wants to restore the walls and gates of your life to make you strong in Him again.

For Speaking Engagements or Questions
Contact
Susan Marie Pender
Susanmariepender@gmail.com
www.lilyofthevalleyhealing.com

www.ingramcontent.com/pod-product-compliance
Lightning Source LLC
Chambersburg PA
CBHW032138040426
42449CB00005B/293